ISRAEL REDEEMED

ISRAEL REDEEMED

Inspiration for the Jewish Festivals

by
RABBI DOV BEGON

Foreword by
Rabbi Menachem Listman

Edited by
Rabbi Menachem Weinberg

URIM PUBLICATIONS
Jerusalem • New York

Israel Redeemed: Inspiration for the Jewish Festivals
by Rabbi Dov Begon

Translations by Raphael Blumberg
Foreword by Rabbi Menachem Listman
Edited by Rabbi Menachem Weinberg

Typeset by Ariel Walden

Printed in Israel

First Edition

ISBN 978-1-60280-433-3

Urim Publications
P.O. Box 52287
Jerusalem 9152102
Israel

www.UrimPublications.com

Cover photo by Alexander Yovenko

Library of Congress Cataloging-in-Publication Data in progress.

Dedicated by

Yehuda Leib Berren *z"l*

In honor of

Rabbi Dov Begon

On the occasion of his Eightieth Birthday

And in appreciation of the

Machon Meir
English Department

Rabbanim, staff and students

In loving memory of

יהודה לייב בן אהרון יצחק ברן ז״ל

Yehuda Leib (Gerald Laurence) Berren

Zikhrono Livrachah

may his memory be a blessing

Born in Boston, Massachusetts

Made Aliyah to Israel in 5771 (2011)

Brought to rest

in the hills of Jerusalem

ח׳ מרחשוון התשפ״א

8th Marcheshvan 5781 (26/10/20)

Table of Contents

Foreword

"THIS IS THE DAY OF THE LORD,
let us exult and rejoice upon it." (Psalms 118)

It is truly a joyous event to present to the English speaking public for the first time this collection of Torah insights, *Torat Eretz Yisrael* – the Torah of the Land of Israel. Our Sages teach us that "there is no Torah like the Torah of Eretz Yisrael" (Bereshit Rabah 16:4). The return home of the people of Israel after 2000 years of exile has brought about a Divine phenomenon, the return of Torah study to Yerushalayim, fulfilling the prophet Isaiah's words, "For from Zion will the Torah come forth and the word of Hashem from Yerushalayim" (Isaiah 2:3). The heart of this revived *Torat Eretz Yisrael* focuses on a tri-part harmony that reflects the inner unity between our nation, our Land and our Torah. I feel certain that Jews around the world, who seek guidance and perspective to appreciate and understand the historic upheavals and glorious successes that the Jewish people are experiencing this century, will find this work invaluable.

Rav Begon was a close *talmid* of Rav Tzvi Yehuda Kook of blessed memory. Throughout his rich career he has spread the light of love and dedication to *Am Yisrael*, *Eretz Yisrael* and *Torat Yisrael*. Over forty years ago he founded Machon Meir to offer students from Israel and around the world a gateway to Jewish observance in the spirit of Rav Kook, and has stood at the helm to this day, as we join to celebrate and honor him upon his 80th birthday.

This collection of Torah insights is culled from years of educational and inspirational messages by Rav Begon, which were published weekly in *Be-ahavah ube'emunah* (With Love and Faith), the Hebrew publication distributed in synagogues throughout Israel, and on the Arutz Meir website and TV station. To honor Rav Begon on the occasion of his 80th birthday, we decided to gather articles that express his unique vision on the Jewish holidays from the perspective of his teachers, *lehagdil Torah ve-le-ha'adirah*, "to increase Torah and to empower it," sharing this wisdom with English speakers everywhere.

Our heartfelt thanks go out to those who were instrumental in this project: For many years these insights were translated with dedication by Raphael Blumberg. Later, our student Zeev Ben Yechiel helped collate the material. Rav Menachem Weinberg envisioned this project and prepared the manuscript for publication. May Hashem grant them many blessings for their valued efforts.

This project was made possible due the generous help of our dear student Yehuda Berren *z"l* who sadly did not live to see the final product. Yehuda's enthusiasm for learning Torah, walking and dancing in the land of Israel, and in the halls of the Beit Midrash, always brought a smile to our faces and endeared him to the students and Rabbis in the yeshiva and beyond.

In addition, Yechiel Zilbershtein deserves recognition for all his help to Yehuda in his last years. We pray that Hashem will grant him strength, good health, and all the blessings of *shamayim* – for his untiring *chesed*, conscientious dedication to learning Torah, and for his part in enabling this *sefer* to reach the Torah community around the world.

Rav Menachem Listman
Director, Machon Meir English Department

Introduction

IN THESE SHORT TORAH INSIGHTS ON THE FESTIVALS, culled from years of educational and inspirational messages, Rabbi Dov Begon, student of Rabbi Tzvi Yehuda Kook *zt"l* and founder of the flagship religious Zionist *kiruv* yeshiva Machon Meir, addresses the unique challenges and opportunities in the historic return of the Jewish people to the land of Israel. Israel's new festivals like Jerusalem Day, Israel's Independence Day (*Yom Ha-atzma'ut*) and Memorial Day for the fallen soldiers of Israel are marked, as well as the *yahrzeits* of the Rabbis Kook – all illuminated by their perspective on Israel's redemption in this age.

Rabbi Dov Begon was educated in the secular kibbutz movement yet was drawn to explore his Jewish heritage. His journey led him to Merkaz HaRav Kook Yeshiva in Jerusalem where he studied for ten years, becoming one of the foremost students of Rabbi Tzvi Yehuda Kook. During the Six-Day War he served as a commander in the Israeli Defense Forces and participated in the liberation of Jerusalem. He forged a new path in the field of *kiruv* and *teshuva*, helping Jews of all backgrounds reconnect with their heritage, uniquely based in the Religious Zionist community in Israel. Shortly after the Yom Kippur War, he founded Machon Meir to assist other Israelis in their first steps toward *teshuva*, and began spreading Torah in the inclusive and passionate spirit of his teachers in all of Israeli society and to students from abroad.

In 5774 (2014) Rabbi Begon was honored with the Jerusalem Worthy Citizen (*Yakir Yerushalayim*) Award.

Machon Meir is a world-class Zionist yeshiva in the heart of Jerusalem. Uniquely it provides an English program within an authentic Israeli yeshiva setting where students from around the world explore meaningful life in Israel and learn Torah tailored for their background. Learn more at http://www.machonmeir.net/ or look for Machon Meir English Department on Facebook. For more information contact english1@emeir.co.il, 02-646-1317 or +972 52-785-1088.

Chapter 1

The Third of Elul: The Yahrzeit of Rav Kook

"God chooses His people Israel with Love."

Rabbi Avraham Yitzchak HaKohen Kook was our visionary leader and shepherd of the nation during this period of national rebirth. His inspiring writings are a prophetic voice which continues to resonate to the present day. Born in 5625 (1865), he passed away on the 3rd of Elul 5695 (1935). Annually, on this day, we commemorate his radiant and lofty soul.

Rav Kook deeply felt the crisis of young Jews abandoning religion, and he devised a strategy to unite the nation and bring estranged Jews closer to their roots, as well as paving a straightforward path through the tangle of relations between religious and secular Jews. The key to his approach lay in understanding the unique nature of the Jewish nation. He distinguished between our active role in fulfilling our mission, versus Israel's inherent chosenness by God: our *segula*.

That *segula*, specialness, is both an inheritance from the Patriarchs, and a reflection of God's having chosen the Jews from all the nations. "You are children of the Lord your God. . . . You are a nation consecrated to the Lord your God. God has chosen you from all nations on the face of the earth to be His own special nation" (Deuteronomy 14:1–2). Rashi comments, "Your sanctity extends from your forefathers. In addition, God has chosen you." Rav Kook expressed this idea when he wrote, "The living light of God burns and shines within every single Jew" (Orot Yisrael 9:6).

Rabbi Meir said, "You are children of the Lord your God: One way or the other, you are called sons. Even when you are foolish, even when you don't believe; even when you worship idols." As the Prophet Hoshea said, "Instead of their being told: 'You are not My people,' they shall be told, 'You are the children of the living God'" (Hoshea 2:1; Kiddushin 36).

Our mission is to live up to this chosenness by doing good deeds and learning Torah. Our success in this regard can change over time, and from person to person. Yet whether we are successful or not in fulfilling our side of the bargain, God's commitment to us as His children remains unshaken. He relates to us in every place and every time with love, as we say in our prayers, "God chooses His people Israel with Love" (blessings of Shema).

In Rav Kook's own words – "Loving our fellow Jew is a by-product of our faith in the divine light of the Jewish people. That light is an inherent characteristic that will never leave the Jewish people. Despite all the vicissitudes of time, it will only become stronger in our midst . . . Most of all, this lofty love has to be aroused amongst the spiritual elite, at a time when the nation's spiritual level is declining, when everything holy is being trampled and religion is being ridiculed. At this time, that spiritual elite must make every effort to discern that despite everything, Israel's spiritual strengths are still enormous. They must gaze at the inner light that penetrates the spirit of the entire nation. That inner light also abides within every individual Jewish soul openly or in secret, and even in a person who has withdrawn far from God's path" (Orot Yisrael 4:2).

Although there are some Jews who are not yet living ethically or practicing mitzvot to fulfill their role as one of God's Chosen

People, with God's help they will eventually choose to connect to their essential goodness.

Today, during this period of national rebirth, the power of this essential nature of the Jewish people is growing stronger and stronger. More and more, the covenant of the Patriarchs is being revealed as an eternal covenant. In our days we are witnessing the fulfillment of the prayer, "God remembers the patriarchs' loyalty, and he brings a redeemer to their children's children for the sake of His name, with love" – through the ingathering of the exiles and the rebuilding of our country, which is developing by leaps and bounds.

A GENERATION DEPRIVED OF LOVE NEEDS LOVE ALL THE MORE

"Say of the righteous man that it shall be well with him, for he shall eat the fruit of his deeds" (Isaiah 3:6).

Rav Kook personified the "righteous man" and our whole generation enjoys the fruits of his labors. In his teachings he sought to teach us how to love the Jewish People precisely "at a time when our people are declining spiritually, when the trampling of what is sacred and the mocking of religion are at their zenith" (Orot 148). Rav Kook explains that "love of our fellow Jews results from faith in the divine light of the Jewish People. . . . Moreover, we must gaze upon that inner light that penetrates the whole community, and whose dwelling place is likewise within every individual Jewish soul, openly or unseen. It even dwells in the soul that has withdrawn far from the path of God" (Orot, Ibid.).

Imagine a child deprived of love because he has misbehaved. In fact, this child actually needs love even more! Rabbi Kook not only expressed these ideas beautifully, he embodied this teaching in his behavior and leadership. He would reach out to those far removed, and like Moshe Rabbenu "descending to the people" he suffered together with them and rejoiced in their happiness. We know that God loves those who love Israel. The greater a person's love of his fellow Jew, the more greatness God will give him.

Today, we must follow the path of Rav Kook, that high priest among his brothers, that grand master in love of the Jewish People. He was a true shepherd for Israel, devoted to his flock, caring and striving for their welfare in every way. He also stood in the breach, insisting on the positive motives behind the behavior of the "sinners of the generation," striving for their atonement. He prayed on their behalf to nullify harsh decrees and to open up for them the gates of blessing.

STAGES OF REPENTANCE

Rav Kook saw with prescience the return to Jewishness of those circles that had distanced themselves from religion and tradition. He noted that the nation would return in four stages. The first stage would be that they would once more show respect for tradition and religion. Out of that respect, they would come to feel affection for religion. Their respect and affection would bring them to study Torah, and only then their respect, affection and study would lead them to mitzvah fulfillment (Orot HaTeshuvah 157).

Rav Kook taught us that this order – respect, affection, study and practice – is the key process to follow as the nation progresses toward redemption. Today we clearly see how the process of the return of those portions of the nation who distanced themselves from tradition and religion is gaining traction. We see how amongst myriads of the Jewish people respect for Jewish tradition is developing. This finds expression within the family and its customs, and in the return to the synagogue on Sabbath and holidays. Even politically, about one fourth of the members of Knesset represent a public that supports tradition and religion. Out of that enormous group that shows respect to religion, there is a group that feels affection for religion and its institutions – they take an interest in Judaism, take part in study groups, attend seminars on Judaism and send their children to religious schools and Talmud Torahs. Out of that group that feels affection for religion and tradition, there is a group that fixes set times for Torah learning in yeshivot and synagogues, and through this, are devoted to mitzvah observance as well.

The return to Judaism can be viewed as a pyramid, at whose base are those who show respect for our faith, and at whose pinnacle are those who study and practice it. All the while, there is great, unceasing movement from the base towards the pinnacle. The day is not far removed when the words of Isaiah 11:9 will be fulfilled: "For the earth shall be full of the knowledge of the Lord, as the waters cover the sea."

Chapter 2

Elul: The Era of Return

IN OUR TIMES THE BIBLICAL PROMISE OF *TESHUVA* IS UNfolding before our very eyes. Through us the Torah's words are being fulfilled:

> "You will then return to Hashem your God, and you will obey Him. . . . Hashem will then bring back your remnants and have mercy on you. Hashem your God will once again gather you from among all the nations where He scattered you. . . . He will then bring you to the land that your ancestors occupied, and you too will occupy it. He will be good to you and make you flourish even more than your ancestors. . . . He will remove the barriers from your hearts and from the hearts of your descendants, so that you will love Hashem your God with all your heart and soul. Thus will you survive" (Deuteronomy 30:2–6).

The repentance the Torah is referring to is a national return – the Jewish People returning to the Land of our life's blood and rising to rebirth. 150 years ago there was a rabbinic mystic named Rabbi Yehuda Alkalai *zt"l*. He was one of the first rabbis, before the rise of modern Zionism, to work for Aliyah and settling the Land, engaging in agriculture and establishing a political entity. Here is what he wrote:

> There are two types of repentance – individual repentance and national repentance. Individual repentance involves a person's repenting his sins. National repentance involves all of Israel returning to the land of our ancestral inheritance, which all the prophets commanded Israel to do, as Rambam ruled: "All the prophets commanded Israel to repent. Israel can only be redeemed by way of repentance" (Hilchot Teshuva).

Rav Avraham Yitzchak Kook, *zt"l*, likewise distinguishes between the isolated repentance of the individual and the repentance of the nation: "The nation's rebirth is the foundation of the great edifice or return, the supreme repentance of Israel and of the entire world which will follow" (Orot HaTeshuvah 17:1).

Today, millions of Jews are returning to Eretz Yisrael. Their very return constitutes magnificent repentance. Isaiah's words, "Return, O Israel, to Hashem, your God" (Isaiah 14:2) are coming to life.

Unfortunately, at present we have not yet reached the fulfillment of the vision of the end of days. We are still weeping and beseeching God, like the kohanim in the days of the prophet Joel (2:17): "Spare Your people, O Lord. Let not Your heritage be the object of contempt, a byword among the nations. Why should the nations ask, 'Where is their God?'" Yet we trust and believe, each day, especially during the days of repentance, that the day is not far off when the prophet's words will be completely fulfilled:

> I will take you from among the nations, and gather you out of all the countries, and will bring you into your own land. And I will sprinkle clean water upon you, and you shall be clean; from all your impurity.... A new heart also will I give you, and a new spirit will I put within you.... I will put My spirit within you.... And you shall dwell in the land that I gave to your fathers; and you shall be My people, and I will be your God (Ezekiel 36:24–28).

As Rabbi Akiva proclaimed, when describing the culmination of these 40 days of repentance, culminating in Yom Kippur – "How fortunate you are, O Israel! Consider before whom you are being purified! Consider Who it is who purifies you" (Mishna Yoma Chapter 8).

THE MONTH OF MERCY

Elul is known as "the month of repentance and mercy." But what is "mercy" of which we are in such great need, in general, and especially at this time? Ramchal (Rabbi Moshe Chaim Luzzatto) explains in his work *Mesillat Yesharim*:

> God rules over His world with "Strict Judgment," responding measure for measure to our deeds. In the way a person conducts himself – that is how God treats him. God watches over everything, large or small, and rewards a person according to his works: "God tells man what [was] his speech" (Amos 3:13) – Even a man's light conversation with his wife is declared to him at his judgment (Avot 1:5). "For God shall bring every work into the judgment concerning every hidden thing, whether it be good or evil" (Ecclesiastes 12:14).
>
> "Strict judgment" means that God judges everything, and that He punishes for every sin we commit – we cannot escape. If God is strict regarding every sin, what then is "mercy"? "Mercy" refers to the continued existence of the universe, for without mercy, the universe could not continue to exist. This trait represents God going beyond the letter of the law.
>
> With Strict Judgment," it would be appropriate for a sinner to be punished immediately upon sinning. Moreover, the punishment would be divine wrath appropriate for someone who rebels against God, and it would be impossible for him to ever rectify his sin. After all, once someone has sinned, once he has murdered or committed adultery, how can he make amends? Seemingly, it is impossible to remove something from existence.
>
> Thus the trait of mercy provides the opposite result of that obtained from "Strict Judgment." First of all, it provides the sinner with time, such that he is not punished immediately. Also, the punishment itself is not carried out with overwhelming wrath. The

> person's rectification, i.e., his repentance, is treated with complete kindness. That is, if someone fully regrets his act and takes upon himself not to repeat it, his uprooting of his will that brought him to sin is then treated as though he had uprooted the deed from existence. It is the same as when one nullifies a vow, where the vow is uprooted from existence. As the prophet said (Isaiah 6:7), "Your iniquity shall be taken away and your sin expiated." The sin is removed from existence. This represents total kindness beyond the letter of the law (Mesillat Yesharim Ch. 4).

God treats His creatures patiently, allowing them an opportunity to make amends, and even goes beyond the letter of the law. We too must follow God's ways. Just as God is merciful, so must we be merciful. Just as He is kind, so must we be kind (Sotah 14b). We must make every effort to make peace with our fellow man. We must make peace within the family, husbands with wives, and children with parents. We must find a way to achieve peace within our nation, without conceding the least bit on the truth of Torah and our belief that Eretz Yisrael belongs only to the Jewish People. Valor and wisdom in life consist of living together despite disagreements. That is how it is in the individual family, and that is how it is within the Jewish People. Through this, may we merit God's mercy in judgment, and through us may the words of the prayer be fulfilled: "Rule over us speedily, O God, alone, in kindness and mercy."

Chapter 3
Rosh Hashanah

GOD HEARS THE SOUND OF HIS PEOPLE ISRAEL'S SHOFAR BLOWING WITH MERCY.

ROSH HASHANAH IS LIKE ITS NAME – THE HEAD (*ROSH*) of the entire year (*shanah*.) Just as a man's head influences his entire person both physically and spiritually, so does Rosh Hashanah influence the entire year. This explains the customs we have on this day, like greeting one another with blessings that we should be "signed and sealed for a good year;" eating apples with honey; and the special wishes we make on Rosh Hashanah night as we eat certain special foods as "signs" or *simanim*. All these customs serve to leave their stamp on the entire year. All of these blessings and wishes are of earthshaking significance, and we mustn't make light of them. Quite the contrary, we must treat a layman's blessing with the full weight due it (Megila 15a).

Rabbi Shneur Zalman of Liadi explained, just as a person has a head and a brain that influence and sustain the entire body, so is Rosh Hashanah a sort of brain for the year, influencing the entire year. And just as one's head, brain and heart have to be pure and righteous, so must we purify ourselves on Rosh Hashanah by way of repentance and good deeds, good thoughts and good speech.

Through this, we influence the entire year, making it good and sweet.

Especially important is the mitzvah of hearing the Shofar (whose very name recalls "improvement" – *shipur*). The Shofar hints and teaches us how we must relate properly and constructively to the Day of Judgment and to strict judgment.

The shofar blasts are blown in sets of three, *teki'ah, terua,* and then another *teki'ah* – and these stages allude to divine kindness, strict judgment and mercy. The first blast, the *teki'ah*, alludes to kindness. It is a simple sound, for where kindness exists, all is simple. In the middle comes the *teruah*, consisting of broken blasts, the sound of loud sobbing, and sighing, weeping and wailing. These allude to strict judgment and to life's hardships. In the end comes another *teki'ah*, a simple blast alluding to mercy and love. Through this pattern we appreciate how the blasts are joined together until one can hear the kindness within strict judgment, the light within the darkness, the sweet within the bitter. We get a sense of how God really is "good to all, with His mercy governing all His works" (Psalm 145:9). Pondering and listening to the sweet, remarkable shofar blasts arouses and strengthens within us the belief that despite everything, when all is said and done, "One higher than the high is watching over us" (Ecclesiastes 5:7), and there is no one else but Him. "The Lord God of Israel is King, and His monarchy rules over all" (Rosh Hashana prayers). In this way a Jew purifies his mind and heart on Rosh Hashanah, and this day shines upon the entire year.

"This year has been a hard and painful one for the Jewish People. The sound of the *teruah*, the sound of weeping and sighing, was the lot of so many innocent Jews expelled from their homes [in Gaza.] The pain and suffering, doubts and worries were the lot of many other Jews as well, who felt the enormity of the pain. On Rosh Hashanah we sing the *piyut* "let the old year and its curses end, and let the new year and its blessings begin." We have to arouse ourselves and grow stronger through the shofar blasts. We have to try hard to hear the *teki'ot* preceding and following the *teruah*. We have to recognize that God, who hears our prayers, mercifully hears the sound of our cries, the *teruah*, as we note in the Rosh Hashanah *amidah*: "Blessed be God . . . who hears the sound of the *teruah* of His people Israel, with mercy."

"HAPPY ARE THE PEOPLE THAT KNOW THE *TERUAH* SHOFAR BLASTS."

On Rosh Hashanah, following the first Shofar blasts, we customarily say, "Happy are the people that know the *teruah* shofar blasts (Psalm 89). They walk, O Lord, in the light of Your countenance." Rav Kook explains, "Happy are the people that know and recognize the efficacy of repentance that derives from the specialness of the shofar blasts, revealed during these days of grace, for rectifying the heart with repentance" (Olat Re'iya II:329).

What is the unique repentance associated with the shofar blasts?

The Torah wrote, "When you go to war against an enemy who attacks you in your land, you shall sound a *tru'ah* on the trumpets. You will then be remembered before the Lord your God, and you will be delivered from your enemies" (Numbers 10:8). Onkelos renders "you shall sound a *tru'ah*" as "*uteyabevun*," meaning that you will ask and cry out for your needs.

In contrast to the weeping sound of the *tru'ah*, the *teki'ah* expresses joy, as it says, "On your days of rejoicing, on your festivals, and on your new-moon celebrations, you shall sound a note [*uteka'atem*] with the trumpets" (10:10). So the process of *teshuva* must start with a *teki'ah*, a simple sound that alludes to the kindness and benevolence that God showers on us, as seen above, "God is good to all, and His mercy is upon all His works"

(Psalm 145:9). Yet at the same time we know that we must follow in His path and rectify our character and deeds through repentance accompanied by weeping, sobbing and wailing – the *tru'ah*. However, once we merit to reach true repentance, we return to the *teki'ah*, this time from great happiness that we have merited the light of God's countenance, as it says, "They walk, O Lord, in the light of Your countenance." At the end of all the blasts comes the *tekia gedola*, the great blast, who teaches us about the complete redemption and complete return that await us in the future.

On Rosh Hashanah we celebrate this joyful *teshuva* represented by the sounds of the shofar. As Rav Kook wrote, this hopeful and heartfelt process is what make us the "happy people" during these "days of grace."

WE ARE ALL EXAMINED TOGETHER

"On Rosh Hashanah, all of mankind pass before God like '*b'nei maron*', as it says, 'God fashions their hearts alike; He considers all their deeds' (Psalm 33:15)" (Rosh Hashanah 16).

Our sages explain that "*b'nei maron*" refers to sheep. That is, on Rosh Hashanah mankind are compared to sheep exiting the compound one by one. When it comes time to take a tithe of the sheep, the farmer does not skip over any one of them.

Some say that "*b'nei maron*" alludes to the climb up to Beit Charon. That climb consisted of a narrow path that people would ascend in single file, with a gaping chasm on either side. Others state that the "*b'nei maron*" were the soldiers of King David. These men were select warriors and they would go forth to battle one by one (Rosh Hashanah 18).

Maharsha explains that these three views that "*b'nei maron*" are either sheep, people climbing up to Beit Charon, or King David's army allude for us to three categories of people, namely evildoers, those in between and the righteous. The sheep allude to evildoers being led off to slaughter. Those who ascend to Beit Charon refer to the people in between, for whom to the right and left lie deep chasms and they walk in the middle. The troops of King David refer to the righteous, who emerge victorious in the war against sin.

Indeed, the Jewish People are composed of *Tzaddikim* (the righteous), *Benoniyim* (those in between) and *Resha'im* (evildoers.) The letters of *tzaddi*, *bet* and *resh* that begin these words form the Hebrew word *tzibbur*, "community." Despite the difference between them, the whole Jewish People are examined together before God. The Creator views their hearts together and "understands all their deeds." God's viewing the Jewish People as a collective on Rosh Hashanah puts their trial in a merciful light, as is hinted at by Genesis 1:31 where Hashem beholds all of creation, "God saw all that He had made, and behold, it was very good."

When we stand before our Creator on Rosh Hashanah, we must recognize and understand that we are not standing individually before the throne of judgment but together with the whole Jewish People, the people God chooses with love. We have suffered so much throughout the generations, and we still remained loyal and clung to God and Torah. May the merit of this, the merit of the fathers and the sons, grant that Hashem protect us and the whole House of Israel in the coming year.

DAY OF REMEMBRANCE

"[On Rosh Hashanah] we recall that the core of Israel's unique spiritual essence is their constantly remembering the content of life and its eternal, enduring spiritual foundation, which embraces the entire universe and enriches it." (Rabbi Tzvi Yehuda Kook, Le'Netivot Yisrael).

Rosh Hashanah is the "Day of Remembrance." On this special day we remember and are remembered. We remember here on earth, and we are remembered On High. We remember that God is King and His kingdom is sovereign over all. We remember on this day that the Master-of-the-Universe, who "sees down through the generations in advance," (Isiah 41:4) chose us, took us out of Egypt and gave us His Torah, and He orchestrates our existence in this generation, in this land, and in Jerusalem.

Not only do we remember, but God remembers as well, as it says, "You will then be remembered before the Lord your God, and will be delivered from your enemies" (Numbers 10:9); and, "The Lord will not cast off His people, neither will He forsake His inheritance" (Psalm 94:14).

We must listen in particular to the shofar blasts, for they possess much content and significance. If someone hears his full measure of shofar blasts, not only will he be awakened from his spiritual slumber of the preceding year, and not only will he improve his deeds and character, but he will be privileged to draw nearer to God. The light of faith will shine in him, the belief that "Hashem the God of Israel is King, and that His sovereignty rules over all" (Rosh Hashana prayers).

"God made man upright" (Ecclesiastes 7:29). In other words, man is essentially good, only that "he seeks out many inventions" (ibid.). Rav Kook taught us that the unceasing distractions of mundane life in this world, complicated by a plethora of calculations, sometimes conceals from us God's benevolent will, which is present everywhere. "For the world is full of God's glory, and His sovereignty rules over all" (Rosh Hashana prayers). The Jewish people, however, are "believers and the sons of believers" (Shabbat 97a). Even when God conceals His countenance, even in situations when we moan and weep, we can realize and see that all is for the best. We therefore end the shofar blasts with another *teki'ah*, the simple blast that alludes to God's traits of kindness and mercy, traits that never cease at any time or under any circumstances, and which are revealed like the sun's shining after a night of darkness.

The shofar blasts relate not only to man as a private individual, but to the general situation of the Jewish People and the entire world. The *teki'ah gedolah*, the long, simple blast at the end, relates to this point, for it alludes to the shofar blast of the Messiah, as we recite each day in the Shemoneh Esreh: "Sound the great shofar for our freedom. Lift up the banner to bring our exiles together, and assemble us from the four corners of the earth."

How fortunate we are to be privileged on Rosh Hashanah to hear the sound of the shofar in the land of our life's blood. The day is not far off when we will merit the coming of the righteous Messiah, and redemption, amidst complete repentance.

Chapter 4

Yom Kippur: A Day of Reconciliation

"THE DAY OF ATONEMENT" IS THE USUAL TRANSLATION for Yom Kippur. However the root of the word *kappara* is given another connotation in Deuteronomy 32:43 "ve*khipper* admato amo." *Rashi* says that the word "*kaparah*" means reconciliation. Rav Kook wrote, "The People and Land of Israel constitute a single essence linked together by a living bond" (Orot 9). So the verse cited can read literally "He will reconcile with His land, His people." "His Land," as well, refers to His people!

Indeed, when the *Kohen Gadol* (High Priest) enters the Holy of Holies on Yom Kippur, to "make atonement [*le-khaper*] for himself, for his family, and for the entire community of Israel" (Leviticus 16:17), his goal is to achieve reconciliation between us and our Father in Heaven, but also between us and our fellow Jews, and with the Land of Israel.

In this era, we are living in the period of God's "reconciling His people to His land," the start of national reconciliation which is finding expression in the ingathering of the exiles, the rebuilding of the Land and the State of Israel.

WHERE THE HOLIEST PERSON, TIME AND PLACE CONVERGE

The Torah teaches us that there are various spiritual levels regarding people, times and places. The *Kohen Gadol* is the holiest person, Yom Kippur is the holiest day of the year, and the Holy of Holies is the holiest place in the world. On Yom Kippur these three pinnacles converge, with the purpose of atoning for the whole community of Israel, and of purifying and sanctifying them.

The farther we advance along the axis of redemption, the spiritual levels of place, time and people will be clarified. It will become more and more obvious that within the Jewish People there are *kohanim* (priests), Levites and Israelites. It will be more and more understood that there are also spiritual gradations within time. Our people will distinguish between the holy and the profane, between the seventh day and the six days of work. They will recognize the holy day Yom Kippur as a day of atonement, of propitiation, purity and holiness.

Finally we will also recognize that there are spiritual gradations within space as well. We will distinguish between Eretz Yisrael and outside the Land. We will recognize the spiritual gradations of holiness within Eretz Yisrael, with Jerusalem being holiest of all. Within Jerusalem there are spiritual gradations as well, up to the highest spiritual level, The Temple and Holy of Holies. By clarifying and recognizing the spiritual gradations within space, time and people, we will increasingly merit the new light that will shine over Zion.

GOD WILL ATONE FOR THE ENTIRE CONGREGATION

Yom Kippur is the day of purification. As Rabbi Akiva said:

"How fortunate you are, O Israel! Before whom are you being

purified? Who is purifying you? Your Father in Heaven! As it says, 'I will sprinkle clean water upon you, and you will be clean' (Ezekiel 35:25). And it also says, 'The Lord is the mikveh [hope, or ritual bath] of Israel' (Jeremiah 17:14). Just as a ritual bath purifies the impure, so does God purify Israel" (Yoma 85b).

All this is particularly relevant on Yom Kippur. As Rambam wrote:

"Yom Kippur is a time of repentance for all, for the individual and for the public. It results in forgiveness for Israel" (Hilchot Teshuva 2:7).

Now it is true that the very essence of Yom Kippur atones, as it says, "This is because on this day you shall have all your sins atoned, so that you will be cleansed. Before God you will be cleansed of all your sins" (Leviticus 16:30). Yet God simultaneously issues us a command. As Rambam wrote: "Everyone is obligated to repent and to confess sin on Yom Kippur" (Rambam, ibid.).

And just as in order to be purified in a ritual bath we have to do a physical deed, to enter the mikveh, so, too, on Yom Kippur we are commanded to confess, and by such means we merit purification, with God's help.

The wording of the confession is entirely in the plural: "May it be God's will . . . that You should forgive us for all our sins and pardon us for all our iniquity and atone for us for all our wrongdoings." We then go on to specify our sins, using a formula organized according to the Hebrew alphabet. When we confess, we have to have in mind not just to confess on our own behalf, but on behalf of everyone. All of Israel are like one body, with one heart. When someone sins, it's not just him! It's also me, for all of us are one people, one soul.

We must learn this lesson from the great rabbis of Israel throughout the generations from our inception as a people until this day. This is an essential idea that the entire Jewish People, and every individual member of it, always bore in their hearts. This explains why the High Priest on Yom Kippur, who would confess for the sins of all Israel: "Aaron shall press both his hands on the live goat's head, and he shall confess on it all the Israelites' sins, rebellious acts and inadvertent misdeeds" (Leviticus 16:21). Because he felt the pain of the collective, and of every individual, and he poured out his heart and prayed to God, he was successful, and "he atoned for the entire people" (verse 24).

The day is not far off when we will be privileged to see the building of the Third Temple and to see *kohanim*, *levi'im* and *Yisraelim* each performing his task in the Temple service. Leading them all will be the *kohen gadol*, the high priest, in the Holy of Holies, praying and atoning for all his people Israel, and blessing them with love.

Chapter 5

Sukkot: The Three Festivals – Seasons of Freedom, Torah, and Joy

THE THREE PILGRIMAGE FESTIVALS, PESACH, SHAVUOT and Sukkot, are one chain linking the Jewish People to their past and their future. They are mentioned in the *Amida* prayer, as "the time of our freedom;" "the time of the giving of our Torah;" and "the time of our rejoicing".

Pesach is the season of our freedom. The Jewish Nation was formed at that time, a unique, exclusive creation of God. As we find in Scripture: "I created this people for Myself that they might tell My praise" (Isaiah 43:21). We were created and we emerged from slavery to eternal freedom, by means of miracles, signs and wonders, God's handiwork for all to see. On Pesach the Jewish People, like a baby emerging from its mother's womb, is revealed as the firstborn son of the Master of the world. They are the nation chosen from amongst all other nations, not just in the past, but also in the present and for eternity. As we recite daily in our prayers: "Blessed are You God, who chooses His people Israel with love."

Shavuot was when we received the Torah. It is not enough to emerge from slavery to political freedom, just as it is not enough to merely be born. Rather, we must develop and uncover the lofty soul hidden in the newborn infant, through providing the child with a fine education and teaching him/her Torah, with love. As our sages said, regarding the giving of the Torah, "Read not that the writing was engraved [*charut*] on the Tablets (Exodus 32:16), but that there was *cherut* – freedom through the Tablets." Just as God blew life into Adam, so He give us the Torah from Heaven at the Sinai Revelation, the same Torah that is the soul of the Jewish People down through the generations. This is the import of the blessing over the Torah *asher bachar banu*, "who chose us from all nations and gave us His Torah." That blessing is not only history, it is a living reality in the present as well, as we say at the end of that blessing in the present tense: "Blessed are You, O Lord, who gives us the Torah." In addition it will be realized for eternity:

> As for Me, this is My covenant with them, says the Lord: My spirit it is which shall be upon you, and My words which I have put in your mouth, shall not depart from your mouth, nor from the mouth of your children, nor from the mouth of your children's children, says the Lord, henceforth and forever (Isaiah 59:21).

Sukkot is the season of our joy. We commemorate that "God caused Israel to dwell in sukkot when He took them out of Egypt" (Leviticus 23:43). Rashi interprets "sukkot" as referring to the clouds of glory (*kavod*.) This signifies a particularly warm and intimate closeness we achieved with Hashem, as He then described "You saw what I did in Egypt, carrying you on eagles' wings and bringing you to Me" (Exodus 19:4). Similarly we find in the *Ha'azinu* song as well "Like an eagle, arousing its nest, hovering over its young, He spread His wings and took them, carrying them on His pinions" (Deuteronomy 32:11). The angels sing of God's glory as we sing in the hymn "*Kel Adon*" – "Grandeur and Glory [*kavod*] they give to His name" and on Sukkot we focus on the fact that we merit to see God's goodness and bask in the splendor of His divine presence.

THE THREE FESTIVALS – PRESENT, PAST AND FUTURE

Only by delving deeply into the historic roots of the Jewish People can we appreciate what we are meriting to see, and gaze ahead to the future that awaits us. The establishment of the Jewish State represents an emergence from two thousand years of exile to political freedom, and it parallels Israel's exodus from Egypt, "the time of our freedom." The return to Torah and to Jewish tradition which is taking place nowadays amongst tens of thousands of our people, both behind the scenes and openly, parallels how we received the Torah at Sinai, and are tantamount to "the time of the giving of our Torah." As we progress toward a renewed spiritual freedom, we will soon merit the completion of the redemption process with the coming of our righteous Messiah and the rebuilding of the Temple, speedily in our day. We rejoice "at the time of our Joy" by dwelling in the sukkah, taking up the four species and reliving the water-drawing festival in the Temple. Then Simchat Torah is the tangible culmination of the process that began with the Exodus, continued with Sinai and the revelation of the divine presence that dwells within us, and has continued to shield and protect us down through the ages.

Particularly on Sukkot we invite into our sukkah the seven *Ushpizin*, honored guests, who also focus our attention to this historic process that goes back to the beginning of our people. We recall the Patriarchs, Abraham, Isaac and Jacob, continuing with Joseph, Moses and Aaron next, and then reach David, King of Israel. Through King David and the Jewish People whom he leads, God's kingdom is ultimately revealed to the world, and to all mankind. As we say in our prayers "[the Jews] will rejoice in Your kingdom."

With such an all-encompassing perspective on the Jewish People through the generations, from our glorious past to our majestic future, we sit in our sukkahs and rejoice. In recent years, as we celebrate Sukkot, millions of Jews have been privileged to celebrate in Eretz Yisrael and in Jerusalem, capital of Israel, multiplying our joy many times over. Ours is not just a private joy, but a national rejoicing.

In the final stage we see that on sukkot the Torah commands us to bring seventy bulls in the Temple as offerings, corresponding to the nations of the world, making Sukkot a holiday that contains a universal theme as well. Ultimately, the prophet promised: "I will bring them to My holy mountain and make them joyful in My house of prayer. Their burnt-offerings and sacrifices shall be acceptable upon My altar, for My house shall be called a house of prayer for all peoples" (Isaiah 56:7).

The State of Israel already today holds an honored place in the family of nations and constitutes a national player with world-wide influence. While today this influence is only in the political, economic and security realms, the day is not far off when all mankind will know and recognize that the Jewish People, living in the State of Israel that is rising to rebirth, are the light of the world morally and spiritually as well. Israel's influence will be recognized for all to see not just because of things written in the Bible in the past, but because we are a nation that lives and breathes the Torah of God in our national and individual lives. We will be a people that sanctifies God's name before all the nations, a people through whom the divine presence is revealed to the entire world.

On Sukkot, Israel's ultimate destiny as a light unto the nations is revealed, hence the enormous joy associated with that holiday. "Make us rejoice in accordance with Your days of afflicting us, the years in which we saw evil" (Psalm 90:15). We will soon be the living fulfillment of King David's words:

"O praise the Lord, all you nations. Laud Him, all you peoples. For His mercy is great toward us; and the truth of the Lord endures forever. Hallelujah (Psalm 117).

THE TREE OF NATIONAL LIFE

In the Sukkah we encounter our nations' forefathers and leaders, Abraham, Isaac and Jacob, Joseph, Moses, Aaron and King David. Each day, another of these faithful shepherds is the guest of honor in our Sukkah and imparts from his benevolent and unique spirit upon the Sukkah dwellers. All of them together, Patriarchs and descendants, find shelter under the wings of the Divine Presence. Just as we reflect upon our ancestors who lived in the early generations and who stand at the foundation of the nation, so do the nation's shepherds have a continued influence upon us.

For the Jewish People are like a tree that has lived for thousands of years. The nation's first leaders and Patriarchs are like the tree's roots, while the generation in which we live is like the branches. The connection and link between the roots and branches, between the Patriarchs and their descendants, between the first generations and recent generations, is critical for our people to continue growing, flourishing and producing sweet fruits. To create the connection between the ancient roots and the new branches, we must provide water for the national tree – and "there is no water but Torah" (Bava Kama 82a). The more the Jewish people today is supplied and "irrigated" with Torah knowledge, the greater will be their connection to the forefathers of our nation, who are our "roots," and their benevolent spirit will ennoble us. The Patriarchs will find joy through us, and with our own eyes we will be privileged to see the fulfillment of the prophecy: "He shall turn the heart of the fathers to the children, and the heart of the children to their fathers" (Malachi 3:24).

SHIELD OF ABRAHAM AND SHIELD OF DAVID

Abraham is called the seed from which the Jewish People have grown. Already at the beginning of his path, God promises him, "I shall make you a great nation" (Genesis 12:2). A growing plant requires protection against all kinds of harmful forces. In the same way, Abraham, his descendants, and his descendants' descendants are protected by God, as in the Amidah prayer, in which we bless God as the "Shield of Abraham."

The great nation that sprang forth from Abraham is the Jewish People, which is growing like an ancient tree whose hoped-for fruit is the Messianic King. The Messiah will come from the House of David and will rule in Eretz Yisrael, bestowing of his benevolent spirit upon the Jewish People and upon all of mankind: "On that day the nations shall seek the root of Jesse that stands as a banner to the peoples" (Isaiah 11:10). Yet King David as well requires God's protection from the enemies, as following the *haftarah* reading we bless God as the "Shield of David."

Despite the noble task assigned to Abraham and to King David – to bring goodness and light to the whole world – the two of them still need shields against those forces and nations who have opposed them and plotted against them throughout history. In the Shemoneh Esreh we therefore mention "*Magen Avraham*" (the Shield of Abraham), and in the Haftarah blessings we mention "*Magen David*" (the Shield of David).

The history of the Jewish people can be summarized as the story of these two shields, the shield of Abraham and the shield of David. It is no coincidence that the emblem on the flag of the State of Israel is the shield of David. This symbol serves to remind us that we live in the period of the ingathering of the exiles and the rebirth of the Jewish nation in the Land of Israel. Despite all the difficulties, God is shielding His people. Particularly in this era when we have been privileged to rise to rebirth in our land, the nations surrounding us scheme against us and attack us. Yet God, the Shield of David, has defended, is defending and will continue to defend the State of Israel, which is the tangible expression of God's having fulfilled His promise to make Abraham a great nation.

On Sukkot we host the "*ushpizin*" guests in our sukkah, consisting of the forefathers of our nation. As mentioned, we start with Abraham on the first day, and end with King David on Hoshana Rabbah, the last day. However there is one more stage represented by Shemini Atzeret and Simchat Torah. After God ensures our success as "a great nation in the Land," we will be privileged to see with our own eyes how all the families of the earth are blessed through Abraham. We hope and pray that in our times, through the rebirth of the Jewish People in their land, an expression of the spirit of the Messiah, we will merit the enormous joy alluded to by the word *hamashiach* ("the Messiah") whose Hebrew letters also create the word *simchah* (joy). As our sages said, "Whoever has not seen the joy of the Sukkot Water-Drawing Celebration has never seen joy his whole life" (Sukkah 51a).

"O Lord, grant us Your holy festivals for gladness and joy. May Israel, who sanctifies Your name rejoice in You" (Festival *Amida* prayer).

Chapter 6
Simchat Torah: Torah with Joy

TWICE A YEAR WE CELEBRATE THE TORAH, ONCE AT Shavuot, the time of God's giving the Torah, and a second time on Shemini Atzeret also known as Simchat Torah.

There is a difference between the two celebrations. On Shavuot, the Jewish people the world over fulfill the custom of "*Tikun Leil Shavuot*" – they learn Torah all night. Of course like all festivals there is an element of happiness, but the joy is relatively restrained. In contrast, on Shemini Atzeret – Simchat Torah, the joy bursts forth, and the Jewish people dance in endless circles, rejoicing with enormous happiness in the synagogues, streets and town squares.

What is the reason for these different expressions of joy? Our sages teach that at the initial giving of the Torah commemorated on Shavuot the Torah was forced upon us:

> "They stood at the foot of the mountain" (Exodus 19:17): This teaches that God overturned the mountain upon them like a barrel and said to them, "If you accept the Torah, well and good. Otherwise, there will be your burial place" (Shabbat 88a).

Anything that comes about through coercion and not through free will, can engender only limited joy. On Simchat Torah, however, all of Israel are celebrating having completed the entire Torah that they read on Shabbat throughout the year, happily and of their own free will, and so exuberant joy is only natural.

"How fortunate we are and how good is our portion") the morning prayers). In our day each year the circles of Jews throughout the Land who rejoice over our holy Torah are increasing. The Torah is returning to its natural abode. "There is no Torah like the Torah of Eretz Yisrael" (Vayikra Rabbah 13) – our land has become the world Torah center, with thousands of yeshivot and educational Torah institutions which are growing and developing everywhere.

When our sages set out to describe what is going to occur in the time of the complete redemption, they mention the enormous joy that will characterize the national and international mood.

"All the days in which Israel were in exile and the light did not shine upon them, that light that they deserved during those days was not lost. Rather, all of it will emerge at once, and then will come a time of rejoicing for Israel, such as there never was. No longer will there be sorrow and sadness in the whole world" (Rabbi Moshe Chaim Luzzatto, Ma'amar HaGeula 1).

"Make us rejoice as in the days when You afflicted us, the years in which we saw evil" (Psalm 90:15). At that time, God will bring joy to His world and will rejoice in the beings He created, as it says, "Let the Lord rejoice in His works" (Psalm 104:31).

The day is not far off when through us will be fulfilled Isaiah's words, "The earth shall be full of the knowledge of the Lord, as the waters cover the sea. . . . For out of Zion shall go forth the law, and the word of God from Jerusalem (2:4 , 11:9)."

Chapter 7
Chanukah: Publicizing the Miracles

THE ESSENCE OF BOTH RABBINIC HOLIDAYS CHANUKAH and Purim is to publicize the miracles and wonders that God did for us in those times, and that He does for us in our own times as well.

On Purim we publicize the miracle of God saving the Jewish People from physical destruction. Wicked Haman sought to annihilate all the Jews, young and old, men, women and children, reminiscent of recent similar attempt by the Nazis in Germany and Poland, yet in the Purim story God protected us, and nullified their plot. On the contrary, Haman and his sons were hung. To remember this physical salvation, we eat and drink on Purim, thereby publicizing that the Jewish corpus lives on and endures despite "Hamans" in every generation.

On the other hand, the wicked Greek regime of the Chanukah story wished to extinguish the soul of the Jewish People. They sought to "make them forget God's Torah and to make them violate the laws expressing God's will" (Al HaNisim prayer). God protected us in our time of trouble, handing over the "evildoers into the hands of the righteous and the wicked into the hands of those who study Your Torah" (Ibid.). To remember the miracle of God saving the Jewish soul, we light Chanukah candles, for "man's soul is the candle of God" (Proverbs 20:27). We thereby publicize that the soul of the Jewish People shines forever within every Jew and within every Jewish home. Thus, the Talmud states, "The mitzvah of Chanukah consists of a candle, for each man and his home" (Tractate Shabbat).

Those same forces that operated in the past are active today as well. Unfortunately, there are still anti-Semitic forces lifting their heads in the world. Their goal is akin to that of wicked Haman, the Nazis in Germany and the Communists of the U.S.S.R. during the Stalinist period. We know that none will succeed with their plot. As the Prophet Isaiah said (Isaiah 54:17), "No weapon formed against you shall prosper, and every tongue that shall rise against you in judgment, you shall condemn."

We are commanded to defend the Jewish People from them, not just in Israel, but throughout the whole world, by means of a strong army, and by means of our people all uniting and standing strong on behalf of our national and Jewish survival. It is a mitzvah to publicize the miracle of God's having saved Israel in our generation. First of all, He established the State of Israel. Second of all, our enemies have attacked us a number of times, with great and mighty forces, but with God's help we have defeated them.

However the ancient Greek threat to extinguish the soul of the Jewish People, through distancing the Jews from their Judaism, by "making them forget their Torah," unfortunately still exists as well. Millions of Jews in Israel and throughout the world are far from Judaism and from the Torah. This weakens their identity and their link to the Jewish People and to the State of Israel. It is not enough to defeat Israel's enemies on the battlefield. We must also increase the light of Israel – the light of "love and faith," the Torah, which is compared to light, as in Proverbs 6:23: "For the mitzvot are a lamp, and the Torah is light." To counter such attempts to "make them forget Your Torah and transgress the laws of Your will" (*al ha-nissim* prayer) we must increase the quantity and quality of Torah learning amongst the Jewish People, and the return to Jewish roots.

With the help of God, here too a miracle is being performed for us like the one in the Second Temple. At that time the Greeks contaminated all the oils. When a single jar of oil was found with the stamp of the High Priest, it sufficed to light the Temple candelabra for eight days even though it actually only contained enough in it for one day. The same has occurred in our own generation. We bear witness that a pure jar of oil is hidden within the heart of every single Jew, whoever he may be, which foreign influences have not succeeded in contaminating. This is being revealed more and more every day, shining additional light upon all of our souls. Tens of thousands of Jews from all walks of life are returning to their roots, returning to the Torah, returning to the synagogue and to Jewish tradition. Just as a person's soul is likened to a candle, as it says, "God's lamp is the soul of man" (Proverbs 20:27), so too, the nation's soul is like a lamp shedding God's light upon the world. Despite all of their efforts, the nations have not succeeded, nor will they succeed, in extinguishing the light of Israel, "for You swore to him in Your name that his light will never go out" (*Haftarah* Blessings).

In addition, on Chanukah itself we publicize two different miracles, the more natural one of Matityahu's military victory over the Greeks, and the supernatural one of the flask of oil, whereby a little oil lasted eight days rather than just one. These two miracles are linked to each other. The former, the Maccabee's military victory, was the result of the self-sacrifice, boldness and determination shown by Matityahu and his sons, undeterred from attacking an enemy militarily stronger and greater than they. These traits earned them divine assistance, and they merited an enormous victory – which then brought about the supernatural miracle of the flask of oil. In that miracle we merited to see

God's supernatural conduct in the form of the candles that burnt above and beyond their natural limits.

For thousands of years the Jewish People have been lighting Chanukah candles. Even in the darkest times when we were at a spiritual low, deep in the darkness of the exile, the Jews did not cease to light Chanukah candles, remembering the supernatural miracle. These candles teach us about the eternity and endurance of the Jewish People, in every time and place. In so doing they demonstrated the supernatural essence of the Jewish People, the people of eternity. The miracle through natural means, the Maccabee's victory over the Greeks, was not emphasized in our sages' words in the darkness of the exile. Today, however, when the Jewish People are rising to rebirth and waging wars against its enemies, it is time to pay attention to this kind of miracle as well.

Remarkably, the symbol of the State of Israel is the seven-branched candelabra. This is a hint to us to recognize the miracles and wonders that God is performing for us in our generation, just like the Purim and the Chanukah miracles. The day is not far off when the Temple will be rebuilt and we will merit to see the actual Temple candelabra, which will shine for us and for the whole world. This Menorah will not just be a symbol of spiritual light but a tangible object, whose candles will offer "testimony to mankind that the Divine Presence rests upon Israel" (Shabbat 22b).

SPREADING THE PURE LIGHT

The Talmud states (Shabbat 21b), "To fulfill the mitzvah of Chanukah, each man and his family must light one candle per day." We are commanded to light a Chanukah candle not just for ourselves but also for our families, and not just for our families, but "place it outside, at the entranceway to our house" (Ibid.).

That is, we must publicize the miracle even for those outside in the public thoroughfare. We must remember that we are commanded to spread light via the Chanukah candles, but no less through our own shining demeanor. Every man and his family, and indeed, every single individual, is commanded to bring light to his surroundings through the sanctification of God's name resulting from his behavior and attributes. We must all increase the light of love and faith, the light of Torah, everywhere.

The first light that the Hasmoneans lit was lit from the pure oil found in the Temple bearing the seal of the *Kohen Gadol* (high priest). Only light with the seal of the *Kohen Gadol* is worthy of bringing light to all of Israel, just as it is the *Kohen Gadol* who atones for all of Israel. Today too, it is not just in our private homes that we must light candles. In our national home as well, we must light many lights of love, of faith and of Torah. We must increase the light we give off in our dealings with our fellow man. After all, we are all brothers.

Our generation very much needs the pure oil bearing the stamp of the *Kohen Gadol*, the great *kohen* who had the capability of bringing light to the whole nation. That man, who left us his pure, illuminating oil, was Rabbi Abraham Isaac Kook, of blessed memory, a *kohen*, and the first Chief Rabbi of Israel. His teachings are like "the precious oil upon the head, running down upon Aaron's beard, running down over the hem of his garments, like the dew of Hermon descending upon the mountains of Zion, for there the Lord has commanded the blessing of everlasting life" (Psalm 133:2–3). We are thrilled to see that those who study and shine the light of Rav Kook are increasing in number everywhere, just as we add new light each night of Chanukah.

Through this we will merit fulfillment of the concluding verse of that psalm "How good and how pleasant it is for brothers to dwell together in unity" (Ibid. v. 1). Ultimately we will all be privileged together, the whole house of Israel, to the new light that will shine upon Zion, filling the Land with knowledge of God, "... like water that covers the sea."

THE SOUL OF CHANUKAH

The Eighth day of Chanukah is known as *Zot Chanukah*, for we read the section in the Torah beginning with the word *Zot* – "This is the dedication of the altar" (Numbers 7:84). However the more famous *Zot* refers to our Torah, as our sages taught: "'*Zot*' can only connote Torah, as it says, 'This is the Torah that Moses placed before the Israelites'" (Deuteronomy 4:44; see Avodah Zarah 2b).

The number seven alludes to finite time, as in the seven day week. The number eight alludes to the dimension of eternity, for it symbolizes a day beyond Shabbat, transcending the usual cycle of time. The Hebrew word for eight (*shemoneh*) has the same letters as the Hebrew word for "soul" (*neshamah*). Hence the eighth day of Chanukah is its soul and essence. Moreover, Torah, linked to Chanukah by the dual use of the word *zot*, is likewise the soul of the people of Israel, the eternal nation.

On Chanukah we must all light Chanukah candles, but when the Temple stood, the Temple was like an enormous atomic power station bringing light to the whole country. The whole Jewish People would unite through the Temple. The Talmud, quoting from Song of Songs 4:4, called the Temple *talpiyot*, "a *tel* (hill) to which all *piyot* (mouths) turn in prayer." From the Temple went forth the light of Torah to all. As Isaiah said (2:3), "Out of Zion shall go forth the Torah, and the word of God from Jerusalem."

Now, that the Temple has been destroyed and remains in its state of ruin, that central spiritual power station lies idle. Only our "miniature Temples" remain, in the form of synagogues and study halls. Hence, every Jew must "light his own candle," illuminating his soul through Torah, mitzvot and good deeds, "for God's commandments are a candle and the Torah is light" (Proverbs 6:23).

Yet "we are believers, the sons of believers" (Shabbat 97a). We are sure that the day is not far off when the Third Temple will be rebuilt. God will then renew our days as of old, and once more, by means of God's chosen Temple, the light of Torah and faith will shine as a beacon for us and for the whole world. We live in the remarkable period of the ingathering of exiles and the rebirth of the Jewish People in their land. All of this can be seen as a preparation, laying the groundwork for the building of the Third Temple. With God's help we will soon be privileged to see with our own eyes the return of the priests to their service in the Temple and the Levites to their singing, and the Israelites to their station, as in ancient times. And may we merit that "a new light will shine upon Zion."

Chapter 8

Tenth of Tevet: The Siege on Jerusalem – Then and Now

On the Tenth of Tevet, Nebuchadnezzar, King of Babylonia encircled Jerusalem and brought it under cruel siege, resulting in the destruction of the First Temple. For that reason, we have a public fast on that day. Kitzur Shulkhan Arukh (121:1) reads:

"We have a positive command from the prophets to fast on days in which troubles befell our ancestors. The purpose of such fasts is to arouse our hearts, to make us vigilant regarding paths to repentance. The fast is supposed to remind us of our evil deeds, and the deeds of our ancestors which were like our own deeds now and which ultimately brought those troubles upon them and us. By remembering these things, we can repent and improve."

In our own generation, the generation of Holocaust and rebirth, the Chief Rabbinate has decreed that the Tenth of Tevet shall also be a day of remembrance for reciting the *Kaddish* in memory of those Jews murdered by the Nazis whose day of death remains unknown.

There is a deep connection between these two painful events in Jewish history – the destruction of the Temple and the Holocaust. Both Nebuchadnezzar and the enemy of the Jews from

Germany both wished to snuff out the light of Israel from the world. In Jerusalem, in the Temple, God chose to reveal Himself and to reveal His light and blessings to Israel, and through them to the entire world. Nebuchadnezzar thought that through the destruction of the Temple, which is like the heart of Israel and the heart of the world, he would succeed in extinguishing the light of Israel, yet he was wrong.

He did not understand that the Jewish People, the people God chose from all nations and that he called His "firstborn son Israel" (Exodus 4:22), were immortal, the eternal people. Although during our long exile we became somewhat like the "dry bones" in Yechezkel's prophecy, the light of Israel cannot be extinguished, even when they are in the nadir of the exile. "The eternity of Israel shall never fail" (I Samuel 15:29).

On the Tenth of Tevet we must remember that in some ways the siege on Jerusalem is still in force, and is even becoming more severe. Not only are our external enemies tightening the siege on Jerusalem, some of our own leaders from within are threatening our capital and country as well. They are under the tragic illusion that if we allow the Arabs to establish an independent state, stealing the land of our life's blood, this will bring Israel peace.

This dangerous mistake stems from a lack of awareness and understanding of the identity and purpose of the Jewish People. This shortcoming is the result of ignorance regarding the tradition and history of our people. Let us hope that all those who are misled will return to their Jewish roots, and will understand the enormity of their error. Instead of establishing a state for the Arabs, they should strengthen our hold on Eretz Yisrael in general and on Jerusalem in particular. It is the task of leadership to strengthen the people's spirit, to bring them back to their roots and enable them to stand proud, recognizing their irrevocable right to their entire land, and the virtue, worth and holiness of Jerusalem.

In our generation, we need to rectify three areas in which we sinned in the past:

1. Torah Learning: Torah learned in a "Hellenistic" or "scientific" manner, without the fear of God and without faith, does not illuminate the soul of those learning it. Our holy Torah constitutes light, as it says, "For *mitzvoth* are a candle, and Torah is light" (Proverbs 6:23). We must attract more Jewish children to reverent Torah study, the sort engaged in by our ancestors. Then, the Torah's light and joy will benefit our entire nation, and the entire world.
2. Ezra and Nechemiah were the leaders who brought Israel out of the Babylonian exile to establish the Second Temple. When they died, the Jewish People were like sheep without a shepherd. Today, we have a great need of leaders like Ezra and Nechemiah, who can strengthen the nation's spirit and unite them. We need leaders who with their great faith can bring light to Israel and can arouse them to return to their roots. In this way all of Israel will come to recognize who we are as a nation, how special we are, and what Israel's role is in general, particularly regarding Eretz Yisrael.
3. The Siege on Jerusalem: Just as in the past Nebuchadnezzar placed a siege on Jerusalem, today, as well, the Arabs and many nations of the world are gazing covetously on Jerusalem, the heart of our nation and the heart of the world, with the goal of extinguishing the light of the universe. We must quash their attacks and their pressure by rebuilding Jerusalem and increasing its population. We must proclaim, "If I forget you, O Jerusalem, let my right hand lose its cunning" (Psalm 137:5), and stand together as one, with one heart, against our enemies besieging Jerusalem. By strengthening and unifying ourselves, loving truth and peace, these days will be transformed to days of joy and gladness and the words of the prophets be fulfilled through us:

"The fast of the fourth month, the fifth month, the seventh and the tenth, shall be to the house of Judah joy and gladness and cheerful seasons. Therefore love truth and peace" (Zechariah 8:19).

Chapter 9

Tu Bishvat: The Sweet Fruits of the Land – a Sign of Redemption

WHAT IS THE SIGN OF ISRAEL'S REDEMPTION? RABBI Abba said that we have no clearer sign than that of Ezekiel 36:8: "But you, O mountains of Israel, shall shoot forth your branches and yield your fruit to My people Israel; for they will soon be coming." Rashi explains: "When Eretz Yisrael yields its fruit bountifully, the end will be near, and we have no clearer sign of redemption" (Sanhedrin 98).

At the height of the kingdom of Israel when the first commonwealth was flourishing in Eretz Yisrael, King Solomon said, "I planted vineyards, I made gardens and orchards, and I planted trees in them of all kinds of fruits" (Ecclesiastes 2:4–5).

Almost all the fruits of the world are found in Eretz Yisrael, because Eretz Yisrael has all the types of soil: "Out of Zion, the perfection [*michlal*] of beauty" (Psalm 50:2). All beauty is included (*kalul*) in it (Yoma 54a).

The custom that Jews eat the fruits of Eretz Yisrael on Tu Bishvat has taken root. In so doing we demonstrate our love and affection for the Land, thereby effecting a great spiritual improvement in the world. When we taste of the enormous assortment of fruits that grow in our land today, there is almost no fruit on earth that cannot be found here, as in the days of King Solomon. We must show our gratitude to God, who is renewing our days as of old, for the fact that Eretz Yisrael is yielding its fruit bountifully to the People of Israel. Following two thousand years of exile, they are now gathering together by the millions – "how fortunate we are and how good is our lot," that we are privileged to see all of this with our own eyes!

THE TREE OF LIFE AND THE TREE OF KNOWLEDGE OF GOOD AND EVIL

On Tu Bishvat, many Jews have a custom of planting trees throughout our beloved land. We find an allusion to this custom in our sages' words:

"From the beginning of the world's creation, God dealt first with planting, as it says, 'God planted a garden in Eden' (Genesis 2:8). You, as well, when you enter the Land, must first engage in planting, as it says, 'When you come to the Land, plant trees bearing fruit' (Leviticus 19:23)." (Vayikra Rabbah 25:3)

Our sages teach us that we have to follow in God's footsteps. Just as God planted a garden in Eden, so must we plant trees in Eretz Yisrael. Yet it is not enough just to plant. We must also tend to what we have planted. Just as God left man in Eden to work and preserve what he planted, so are we commanded to cultivate and preserve our public and private lives here. Otherwise, we are liable to ruin the Garden of Eden in which we live. As our sages said:

"When God created Adam, He took him around and showed him all the trees in Eden, and He said to him, "Observe how fine is My handiwork. Everything I created, I created for you. Be careful not to ruin and destroy My world!" (Kohelet Rabbah 7)

In addition, Adam was commanded not to eat from the Tree of Knowledge of Good and Evil. Eating from the tree brought shame and sadness to Adam and to all mankind for whoever ate from that tree would imagine that only he knows what is good and what is evil, and consequently he would ignore Divine instruction that teaches us what is really good and what is really evil. As we sing whenever we accompany the Torah scroll, the Torah is a "tree of life for those who take hold of it."

So while we appreciate and celebrate the flourishing of Jewish agriculture in the land of Israel we must take care to cultivate and preserve these roots in our holy, beloved land. We must develop our land and settle throughout its length and breadth, guarding it from the enemies, robbers of our land, whose entire goal is to destroy the State of Israel.

Above all else, we must be careful not to "eat the Tree of Knowledge of Good and Evil." We mustn't think that good and evil in our private and public lives depend only on our own judgment. Those who hold the reins of government must be especially careful to avoid this mistake. We must all realize that good and evil, as far as our hold on Eretz Yisrael, are learned from our holy Torah. That is the moral basis for us and for the nations of the world that justifies our possession of the Land of our life's blood. As Rashi explains at the start of the Torah, should the nations come and call us thieves for having conquered Eretz Yisrael, we must answer them, "God told His people of His might, in giving them the inheritance of nations" (Psalm 101:6).

Chapter 10

Purim and the Yahrzeit of Rav Tzvi Yehuda Kook: Joy in Trying Times

"When Adar arrives we increase our joy, and when Av arrives we decrease our joy" (Ta'anit 29a).

In Adar, God shone His countenance upon us and saved us from the plot of wicked Haman. We therefore display great joy over God's enormous kindness. Yet even in Av, during which God concealed His countenance from Israel and two Temples were destroyed, we do not eliminate our joy altogether but only "decrease" it. The foundation of our faith is that even when God "conceals His countenance," our Father in Heaven is still acting in secret for our benefit. Therefore, a believing Jew who truly, constantly serves God, must remain joyous, whether God is revealing His face or concealing it. Joy may be compared to music. The volume can be turned up or down, but the tune of faith, trust and joy cannot be turned off altogether. "A person must bless God for the bad just as he blesses Him for the good" (Brachot 9). R. David Kimchi rejoins "with a whole heart and with joy" (Redak, I Samuel).

The State of Israel finds itself in a complex and complicated situation. We are at war with our enemies who are rising up to destroy us and to drive us out our land – it will never be! Likewise, cultural, social and political power struggles from within are seemingly weakening the strength and fortitude of the nation. Even so, we trust in God, and rely on the words of our prophets, prophets of truth and justice: "The Lord will not cast off His people, nor will He forsake His inheritance" (Psalm 94:14). The farther we march along the upward path to complete redemption, the greater will be the joy of Israel and the whole world. Ultimately we will see with our own eyes how "the nations shall cease from God's land" (Psalm 10:16); and "the Lord shall bring the counsel of nations to naught, and make the people's devices to be of no effect. The Lord's counsel shall stand forever; the thoughts of His heart for all generations" (Psalm 33:10–11).

SHABBAT ZACHOR: "THE JEWS HAD LIGHT AND GLADNESS, JOY AND HONOR."

The Sabbath before Purim it is a mitzvah to read "*Parashat Zachor*" (Deuteronomy 25:17–19), to remember "what Amalek did to you on your way out of Egypt." How should we understand what it is that they did? "When they encountered you on the way, and you were tired and exhausted, they cut off those lagging to your rear, and they did not fear God" (ibid 18). Amalek wished to show all the nations that Israel is merely a "nation like all other nations." Rashi comments:

"'When they encountered you [Heb.: *karcha*] on the way': The meaning is 'cold' [*kar*] as opposed to heat. They cooled you down to lukewarm temperature from boiling heat. For all the nations were afraid of waging war against you, until they commenced, preparing the way for others. This is compared with a boiling bath into which no one could enter. One villain came and leaped into it. Although he was scalded, he cooled it for the others."

Amalek's gross impudence in fighting Israel immediately after the Exodus and the splitting of the sea, when all could see that Israel are exalted over all other nations, and God's special favorite, was made possible as a result of the weakness that reigned over Israel, as it says, "Amalek came and fought Israel at Rephidim" (Exodus 17:8), which our sages interpret to mean "the place where Israel grew lax [*raphu yedeihem*] in Torah learning." At Rephidim, their faith and identity were weakened, and they said, "Is God in our midst or not?" (Exodus 17:7).

Israel's victory over Amalek was rendered possible by Moses and Joshua exalting and strengthening the spirit of the nation and their faith, as it says, "When Moses would lift his arm, Israel would prevail" (Exodus 17:11). Our sages ask: "Did Moses's arms make or break the war? Rather, the point is that as long as Israel gazed upward and subjugated their hearts to their Father in Heaven, they would prevail. Otherwise, they would fall" (Rosh Hashanah 29a). Moses, in raising his arms upward, was hinting to Israel that Amalek's goal was to defeat Israel, which would constitute a profanation of God's name. After all, God's name was called upon us, Israel's wars are God's wars, and Israel is God's army.

The goal of the Amalekites of the past, and those who have followed in their path through the generations until today, is to show everyone that Israel is like all the nations and can be fought and humiliated, and even annihilated, as Haman and Hitler tried to do. In our very day as well, the Arabs who seek to steal our land, and their Muslim supporters, have the same goal.

In face of this goal of humiliating Israel and blurring their identity and national purpose of bringing light to the world from Eretz Yisrael, we have to place at the head of our country a leadership that recognizes the identity and uniqueness of the Jewish People – a leadership that will broadcast faith and trust in the righteousness of our historic and divine right to our land. It has to be a leadership that will deter our enemies not only with weaponry and a strong army, but with a profound spirit and strong faith. It has to be a leadership that will unite the nation, and that will call out with a loud, clear voice, both to our people and to the whole world, that the Lord God of Israel is King, and is sovereign over all, and that He chose us from among all nations and gave us His Torah and Land. By such means may we be privileged to see with our own eyes how the tables are turned, how the Jews will have "light and gladness, joy and honor (Esther 8:16).

THE YAHRZEIT OF RABBI TZVI YEHUDA KOOK

On the 14th of Adar, the first day of Purim 5742 (1982) our teacher and master Rabbi Tzvi Yehuda Kook was taken to the celestial sphere. All his life he engaged in disseminating the Torah lights of his father. Those lights have spread a good and pleasant fragrance to the entire House of Israel and to the entire world. Rav Tzvi Yehuda was privileged to be the great educator who actualized the potential of his father's blessed light and raised up numerous disciples who follow in his light.

Rav Tzvi Yehuda would customarily explain our sages' words, "The sanctification of God's name is greater than the Profanation of God's name (*me'chillul Hashem*)" as meaning, "The greatest sanctification of God's name is one that emerges from the profanation of God's name." When a believing person merits to ascend in Torah greatness, and in the fear and love of God, he merits to see with his spiritual sight how truly everything is for the best. Then, even what seems at the time like the profanation of God's name, darkness and evil, turns out to be part of God's kingdom.

And perhaps that is the spiritual level that the person drinking wine on Purim must reach, such that "he cannot distinguish between 'Cursed be Haman' and 'Blessed be Mordechai.'" Both stand beneath the watchful gaze of God, and "everything God does He does for the good."

WHEN THE WINE GOES IN, THE FRAGRANCE COMES OUT.

"A person is obligated to drink [Hebrew: *lehitbasem*] on Purim until he cannot tell the difference between 'Cursed be Haman' and 'Blessed be Mordechai'" (Megillah 7b; Orach Chaim 695:2). Seemingly we can ask: How can our sages require us to drink? Surely drunkenness causes great sin. However this is required to commemorate the miracles performed for the Jewish People on Purim that occurred by way of drinking parties. Vashti was removed from the throne by way of a drinking party, bringing in Esther. Likewise, Haman's downfall came about through a drinking party. Our sages therefore required us to drink enough that we should remember the great miracle by way of wine.

All the same, we are not commanded to get drunk and to allow our reveling to diminish our dignity to the point of rakish foolishness, but only enough to achieve a pleasurable feeling of love for God and thankfulness for the miracles He performed for us. If, however, someone knows about himself that drinking will make him treat one of the mitzvoth lightly, even such as ritual hand-washing or the blessing after the meal, or that it will make him skip the *mincha* or *ma'ariv* prayers or behave frivolously, then he ought to abstain. "All one's deeds should be for the sake of Heaven" (Orach Chaim 695:2, Biur Halachah).

Why do our sages use the Hebrew expression "*lehitbasem*" (literally to have a fragrance) for "to drink," rather than "*lehishtaker*," the normal expression for "to get drunk"? It is because, as our sages said, "When wine goes in, secrets come out" (Sanhedrin 38a). And what are the "secrets" that come out of a Jew who drinks wine on Purim? Only good words leave his lips, and, as our sages said, "'Good' can only mean Torah," or, "'Good' can only mean a righteous person." The opposite occurred at the drinking feast of Achashverosh. There, the king's honorees, gathered together from amongst all the nations, sat and drank a king's share of wine, and their true faces were revealed, all lasciviousness and corruption, the opposite of the pleasant fragrance exuded by the Jewish People even when they drink wine.

Our drinking serves to make us fragrant with the great love between the Jewish people and our beloved. May we merit to be the living fulfillment of Song of Songs 8:14: "Make haste, my beloved! Be like a gazelle or a young hart upon the mountains of spices."

THE SCROLL OF ESTHER – A REVELATION OF GOD'S LOVE

The story of Esther can be seen as a synopsis of the entire history of the Jewish People. At first there are difficulties and complications, with Israel facing terrible threats of extermination, but the conclusion is good and pleasant, with Israel defeating its enemies. Ultimately, The Jews have "light and gladness, and joy and honor" (Esther 8:16).

The name "*Megillat Esther*" (the Scroll of Esther) alludes to these two situations, one (*gilui* – similar to the word *megilah*) of God revealing His countenance to us, and the other (*hester*) of God hiding His face from us. Ostensibly, these two situations are opposites, but in truth, both serve one end – God's revealing His everlasting love to His People Israel. Megillat Esther reveals to us that even when God is concealing His countenance in the darkness of the exile, where we may suffer its terrible tribulations, He still loves us – as we entreat Him daily in our evening prayers, "Never remove Your love from us."

The custom of masquerading on Purim likewise expresses the theme of revelation and concealment. Wearing a costume hides your identity, such that on the outside you look entirely different from what you really are. The mask, however, cannot blot out the face and personality of the one behind it. In the same way, even though God, so to speak, sometimes hides His face from Israel, His love for us and His interest in our welfare endures always. It is precisely like the blessing we recite each morning before the Shema, praising God who "with love, has chosen His People Israel." A few moments later we again affirm that God "shall bring a redeemer to His children's children for the sake of His name, with love" (Shemoneh Esreh).

"GO GATHER TOGETHER ALL THE JEWS" (ESTHER 4:16).

Esther asks of Mordechai, "Go gather together all the Jews." On the surface, Mordechai's mission is to unify all of the Jews, who appear to Haman as "a people scattered and dispersed among the nations" (Esther 3:8). This task seems impossible. Is it really possible to gather together and to unify all the Jews? After all, there are so many differences and so many opinions, so many streams and parties. How is it possible to gather together and unite them all? What is the secret of unity?

From where can we find the strength to gather together and unite the Jewish People? Is it only our fear of Haman's decrees in the past, or threats to the Jewish People in the present that can unite us all? The secret of uniting all of the Jews is to return to ourselves, to return to our roots. The root of a tree is where all the divergent branches unite, and so, too, in the roots of the Jewish People, we can find what unites and binds us. Surely we all possess one Father, and our whole nation has one destiny. It is just that the tree's root is hiding in the ground, and only the branches are visible to the eye.

As above, this is alluded to by the expression "*Megillat Esther*." On the one hand, the word "*megilah*" is linked to the word "*gilui*," meaning "revelation." On the other hand, the word "Esther" is linked to the word "*hester*," meaning "concealment." It is the same with the human body, whose many limbs and organs are visible to the naked eye, whereas the soul, which is hidden, unites all the limbs and organs together. It is likewise the same with the Jewish People. All of us together possess one soul, for all ages.

The more we delve deeply in study to reach this understanding, to clarify and know our roots, going back to our forefathers, Abraham, Isaac and Jacob, the more we will discover what unites us. We will discover ourselves and our private and universal destiny, and we will march together up the winding path to complete redemption, as God promised Abraham, "I will make you into a great nation . . . You shall become a blessing. . . . All the families of the earth will be blessed through you" (Genesis 12:2). Then, all together, we will merit the "new light that will shine upon Zion."

FROM "SCATTERED AND DISPERSED" TO "ONE NATION IN THE LAND"

Purim is different from all the other holidays. While with all the other holidays, the Jewish People unite and celebrate on the same day, on Purim we split up the holiday. During normal years, we split it into two parts: Purim of unwalled towns occurs on the fourteenth of Adar, and Shushan Purim for walled cities, on the fifteenth.

This year we are privileged to have a three-way split in Purim. On the fourteenth, a Friday, we recite the Megillah and give gifts to the poor, even in Jerusalem, which has a wall going back to the days of Joshua. On the Sabbath, in walled cities, we recite "*Al HaNissim*" in both the Shemoneh Esreh and in Grace after Meals. On Sunday, we fulfill the mitzvot of sending food parcels to our fellow man, and the "Purim Seudah," the festive Purim meal.

This splitting up of Purim serves to remind us that we have to publicize for two days the miracle that was performed for us in those days at this time. The first day is for all of the provinces of Ahasuerus's kingdom, and the second day is for Shushan the Capital. For the sake of the Land of Israel's glory, the Rabbis decreed that cities that were walled in Joshua's time should read the Megillah on the same day as in Shushan, namely the fifteenth of Adar, "Shushan Purim" (Orach Chaim 688:1, Mishnah Berurah).

Making the miracle and the holiday last longer by spreading them out over several days serves also as an allusion to us about Israel's plight in the exile. As in the words of Wicked Haman: "There is one people, scattered and dispersed among the nations" (Esther 3:8). True, they are one people, yet they are scattered and dispersed. This by itself is a miracle. Despite their being scattered and dispersed, they remain one people.

Today, we are in the remarkable era of the ingathering of the exiles. We are gathering together in our land, like dry bones growing skin, flesh and sinews. Speedily, it will be revealed to all that we are, indeed, "one nation in the land" (II Shmuel 7:23), solitary and special, just as God is solitary and special. According to the Midrash, God says to Israel, "You have proclaimed Me unique in the world, and I shall make you unique in the world." May we, through coming to know our uniqueness and identity, also come to know our task and mission in our land, and in the whole world.

The entire House of Israel caught a glimpse of this when they saw the reaction of the rabbis of Yeshivat Merkaz Harav and its yeshiva high school, as well as the bereaving families of the holy children murdered by Arabs seeking to steal our land. All of them reacted out of faith and valor, out of an all-encompassing vision of the intricate and complex reality faced by our nation and our country at this hour. How fortunate we are to have been privileged to learn and to teach Rav Kook's lights. We hope that those lights will illuminate the entire House of Israel, and that Israel will bask in their pleasant fragrance.

Chapter 11

Pesach: The Miracle of Shabbat HaGadol

"THE SABBATH BEFORE PASSOVER IS CALLED *SHABBAT HaGadol* [the great Sabbath] because of the miracle that was performed then" (Shulkhan Arukh, Orach Chaim, 430). What was that miracle? The year that Israel left Egypt, the tenth of the month of Nissan came out on a Sabbath. Every Jew took a lamb for his Pascal offering and tied it to the bedpost, as it says, "On the tenth of this month, every man must take a lamb for each extended family, a lamb for each household. . . . Hold it in safekeeping until the fourteenth day of this month. The entire community of Israel shall then slaughter their sacrifices in the afternoon" (Exodus 12:3, 6). The Egyptians saw this and asked them why they were doing this, and they replied, "To sacrifice it for the sake of Passover, following God's command to us." The Egyptians gritted their teeth over the fact that the Israelites were slaughtering their gods, while they, the Egyptians, were not allowed to say anything in response. And because the tenth of the month came out that year on the Sabbath, it was decided that the Sabbath before Passover must always be called "Shabbat HaGadol" (Mishnah Berurah, Ibid.).

According to our sages, the great miracle occurred when the

Israelites bound the lamb and publicized that they were about to slaughter it, despite the Egyptians considering it a god. The Egyptians were unable to speak a word, and they could not touch the Israelites.

The Egyptians worshipped and subjugated themselves to base materialism. They saw in base material the source and purpose of all of life. The surrender to materialism and passion was the chief axis around which the culture of the society and individual in Egypt turned. This animalistic ideology was symbolized by the lamb and the calf. Suddenly up rose Israel, who were enslaved to Egypt, who in turn were enslaved to their passions and their beasts, and Israel slaughtered their deity before their eyes, without the Egyptians being able to protest or touch them. This, by itself, was a great miracle which God performed, still performs, and will perform in the future for the Jewish People forever.

Ramban brings another reason for why the Israelites chose precisely a lamb: It is because the month of Nissan is under the astrological sign of the lamb, and the Egyptians believed in astrology – that is, that everything is under the control of the constellations and nature. They did not believe that there is Someone who is the Supreme Deity, the true Master of all. God therefore commanded that Israel slaughter a lamb and consume it, to make known to Israel and to the whole world that not by the power of the constellations did we leave Egypt, but because of the decree of God, and because of His love for the Jewish People.

On Shabbat HaGadol, even before Passover, we must recall the great miracle that was performed for us. Despite our being a weak, enslaved people in Egypt, we raised up our heads, and the miracle, for all of Egypt to see, was performed for us out of God's love of Israel. Today too, all our enemies will be unable to overcome us, because "He who chooses Israel with love" (Morning prayers) continues with His great love and compassion for the Jewish People.

THE PACE OF REDEMPTION – IN EGYPT AND FOR ALL TIME

The miracle of the Exodus occurred with suddenness, *chipazon*. After hundreds of years of slavery, the redemption came with lightning speed. All at once for all to see, both Israel and Egypt, God's omnipotence was revealed, unlimited by time and space. Everyone saw that when God wishes it, He can redeem us in a moment.

Regarding the Pesach offering it says, "You must eat it with your waist belted, your shoes on your feet, and your staff in your hand, and you must eat it in haste. It is the Passover (Pesach) offering to God" Shemot 12:11)).

Rashi comments:

"The offering is called the '*Pesach*' (Hebrew for 'pass over') because God passed over the Jewish homes amongst the Egyptian homes, skipping from Egyptian to Egyptian, with the Israelites in between being spared. Therefore, you too must perform all the entire service with alacrity, skipping for the sake of God."

The matzot too were first made with haste: "[The Israelites] baked the dough that they had brought out of Egypt into unleavened [matzah] cakes, since it had not risen. They had been driven out of Egypt and could not delay, and they had not prepared any other provisions" (Shemot 12:32).

The miracle of the Exodus occurred with suddenness and with haste, and we consumed the Pesach offering hastily as well, yet our sages teach us that the Pesach offering in the future will not be consumed in haste but slowly and moderately (Pesachim 96a).

In our own generation, the generation of our national rebirth, we must distinguish between miraculous spiritual redemption and a more gradual natural process. The student of Rav Kook, and Rosh Yeshiva of Merkaz Harav, Rabbi Ya'akov Moshe Charlap, taught:

> Since in the redemption from Egypt the fundamental element was the liberation of the spirit, the redemption therefore occurred hastily. Yet as far as the physical liberation, the majority of the nation, with their exilic character, feared everything and wished to return to the exile, saying, "Let us select a leader and return to Egypt" (Numbers 14:4).

The physical redemption may proceed slowly, but will not be followed by additional exile. Regarding the redemption of the spirit in the future redemption, we may expect that it will be hasty as well. Rav Charlap continues:

> "The Lord, whom you seek, will suddenly come to His temple, and the messenger of the covenant, whom you delight in, behold, he is coming!" (Malachi 3:1). Nature advances gradually. Miracles come suddenly. When it comes the turn of the soul to be redeemed, the light of the soul's redemption will suddenly begin to shine and to emanate.... And the sons will return to their Father in Heaven with remarkable repentance, with total love, following the Lord their God and clinging to Him . . . And even those far removed from God and from His Torah will hear and will come to crown God with the crown of kingship (Rav Charlap, MiMa'ayanei HaYeshua 21:4).

"A redeemer will come to Zion, and unto them that turn from transgression in Jacob – the word of God. As for Me, this is My covenant with them – the word of God. My spirit that is upon you, and My words which I have put in your mouth, shall not depart out of thy mouth, nor out of the mouth of your seed, nor out of the mouth of your seed's seed – the word of God – henceforth and forever" (Isaiah 59:20).

WE WERE BORN IN EGYPT AND WE ARE GROWING TO ADULTHOOD IN JERUSALEM.

On the Seder night, all Jews sit together in families, joyously retelling the story of the Exodus, the story of the birth of the

Jewish People and of their being chosen. It is a story that discretely reveals a small share of God's great love and affection for His people Israel, His firstborn son, whom He saved from slavery and took for a people. Thank God, in our day we can tell those present at the Seder that God likewise brought us into the Land that He swore to our ancestors to give to us as an inheritance. We must remember that not only at the Exodus did God love us, but that He loves us every day and every second.

When a baby is born, a fine new soul appears in the world, for "man's soul is God's candle." Yet the joyous parents have their eyes trained on the future as well. They ask: What will be the future of this fine soul when it grows up and matures? How will it be privileged to spread its good, sweet light? We do not suffice with the birth; our eyes are always looking towards the future. It was that way at the Exodus as well. We were born and set apart and redeemed in Egypt. Yet our eyes are lifted towards the future redemption, the redemption towards which our nation and all mankind are heading.

The Jewish People have come a long way over thousands of years since the Exodus. Finally, with God's help, we are meriting to come home to Jerusalem. The Jewish People were born in Egypt, but the revelation of their benevolent soul for all mankind is in Jerusalem, the source of light of the world. That is where the redemption of Israel and the world, which began with Israel's appearance on the stage of history in Egypt, will finally take place. We will merit to continue marching upward along the long path from Egypt to rebuilt Jerusalem, and we will be privileged to see the rebuilding of the Temple. Through us will be fulfilled, "For out of Zion shall go forth the Torah, and the word of God from Jerusalem" (Isaiah 2:4).

COMBINING MATZAH AND MARROR – FREEDOM AND SLAVERY

"Thus did Hillel when the Temple stood: He would combine matzah and marror [bitter herbs] and eat them together to fulfill what it says, 'They shall eat it with matzah and marror' (Numbers 9:11)." (Haggadah)

As is known, matzah recalls freedom while marror recalls slavery. Seemingly, the two are opposites. Even so, Hillel, whose identifying trait was that he "loved peace and would pursue peace, he loved his fellow men and would bring them close to the Torah" (Avot), would combine matzah and marror and eat them. Why?

Rabbi Avraham Yitzchak Kook (Olat Re'iyah 289) explains that we have to view slavery and freedom not as two distinct forces that do not influence each other, but as two forces which are linked together and which complete each other.

Matzah, symbolizing freedom, alludes to Israel's instinctive love of God, His Torah, His mitzvot and His creations. By contrast, marror, symbolizing slavery, teaches us that we have to bring that love from a potential to a reality through our being slaves to the will of God. This is exalted enslavement, enslavement to the King of Glory, which is total freedom. Thus, the perfect form of freedom emerges when it is linked to slavery.

Today, we must learn from Hillel the Elder as we approach reclining on the Seder night as free men. As we celebrate the holiday of freedom, we must tell our children, and ourselves, the remarkable story of our people when they were first born in the darkness of Egypt. We must tell of the miracles and wonders which God performed by dint of His love for His firstborn son Israel. We must tell of Israel's soul, which serves to bring light to the entire world despite the forces of darkness which rise up against us in every generation with the intent of snuffing out the light of the world – it will never be! We must remember that freedom truly demands enslavement, and we must combine the two together, as in the words of Rabbi Yehuda HaLevi (Kuzari 5:205):

"I seek only freedom from enslavement to man. I seek enslavement to One – to God, because enslavement to Him is freedom, and surrender to Him is the true glory."

THE EXODUS NARRATIVE – A LOVE STORY

Pesach (Passover) derives its name from God's great love and compassion for the Jewish People, in His passing over their homes as He smote the Egyptian firstborn. As it says, "I will then pass over you and will not allow the destroyer to enter your houses to plague you. . . . When your children ask you, 'What is this service of yours?' You shall say, 'It is the Pesach-offering to God, who passed over the houses of the Israelites in Egypt when He struck the Egyptians and saved our homes.' The people then bowed and prostrated themselves" (Exodus 12:23–27).

Rashi relates to the Israelites having bowed: "Why did they prostrate themselves and bow? It was in thankfulness for their being told that they would be redeemed, would come into the Land and would bear children."

Their love, faith and trust in God's love for them were so great that they thanked Him by bowing to Him while they were still slaves in Egypt before being redeemed. Such is the way of people who love one another. Their distress and suffering does not stop that love.

Indeed, the Exodus narrative is the story of the great love that abides between God and Israel, as in our daily prayers, where we bless God, who "has lovingly selected His people Israel." We likewise recite in the Shema, "You shall love the Lord your God with all your heart, soul and might." This is not merely a command;

it is a promise. Indeed, we customarily complete the Seder Night by reciting Song of Songs, King Solomon's marvelous, profound poem celebrating the love between God and the Jewish People.

That story of the great love between God and Israel is retold in the Pesach Haggadah from generation to generation, father to son, as we recline as free men on the first night of the holiday. Historically we have faced unimaginably harsh conditions – when we were pursued to death by the Spanish Inquisition, or when Jews were being burned to death in the furnaces of Auschwitz. However, even throughout those times, Jews never ceased to recite, in secret, that great love story. Reciting the Haggadah during our most difficult hours reveals our great love for God. As with all who truly love one another, we love God under all conditions and in all situations.

The Haggadah begins with the words, "We were slaves to Pharaoh in Egypt," and it concludes, "Next year in rebuilt Jerusalem." This is a story going back thousands of years, but it is replete with love.

"The children of Israel emerged [*yotzim*] triumphantly" (Exodus 14:8). Rabbi Tzvi Yehuda Kook, in his talks (Parshat Bo), would stress that the word *yotzim* is in the present tense, and he would say, "We have been continuously leaving Egypt from then until now. Throughout all the generations, we have been leaving Egypt in greater and greater triumph."

We live in a remarkable period, in which God's promise is being fulfilled: "I will bring you to the land regarding which I raised My hand, swearing that I would give it to Abraham, Isaac and Jacob. I will give it to you as an inheritance. I am the Lord" (Exodus 6:8). We have to view all of Jewish history as occurring between two places – Egypt and Jerusalem – and between two personalities – Moses and the Messianic king from the Davidic line – may he come speedily in our day.

How fortunate we are and how good is our lot that in the long journey of thousands of years since the exodus from Egypt, we are near the end of the journey, in Jerusalem. We are not slaves to Egypt and the nations. Rather, we are in our own land, witnessing the rebuilding of Jerusalem with our own eyes.

"We therefore are obligated to thank, praise, laud, glorify, exalt, honor, bless, extol and adore Him who performed for our fathers and for us all of these wonders. . . . Therefore, let us recite a new song before Him." (Pesach Haggadah)

IN THE SONG SUNG AT THE SEA, LEFT BECOMES RIGHT

In the song sung by Moses at the Sea of Reeds, it says, "Your right hand, O Lord, is awesome in power. Your right hand, O Lord, crushes the foe" (Exodus 15:6). Rashi comments, "It says 'Your right hand' twice. When Israel perform God's will, left becomes right."

How can "left" become "right?" "Right" and "left" symbolize, respectively, God's traits of kindness and strict justice. When Israel perform God's will, they are exalted and they merit to see how the trait of kindness is hidden within the trait of strict justice and how kindness is the soul of strict justice, such that strict justice, the "left," automatically becomes kindness, the "right." Indeed, "the deeds of the Mighty One are perfect, for all His ways are just. He is a faithful God, never unfair; righteous and moral is He" (Deuteronomy 32:4). We must try to ascend and reach this exalted perspective, to understand that even all of the complications and difficulties conceal within them the trait of kindness.

Even when God conducts Himself towards us with strict justice, concealing His countenance from us, His intention, desire and purpose is to show us benevolence, for "the Lord is good to all; and His tender mercies are over all His works" (Psalms 145:9). This is especially so regarding the Jewish People, God's beloved children. In Egypt, God conducted Himself towards them with strict justice, with the Egyptians pursuing and persecuting them. Now, at the splitting of the sea, Israel saw clearly how strict justice could be transformed into kindness: "Pharaoh's chariots and army He cast in the sea. His very best officers were drowned in the Sea of Reeds. . . . You made Your wind blow; the sea covered them. They sank like lead in the mighty waters" (Exodus 15:4, 10). Our sages comment, "The mighty enemies and obstacles that had seemed so unbeatable sank like lead, as if they had never existed."

When Israel perform God's will, they merit to see how within the very trait of strict justice is hidden the trait of kindness. At the splitting of the sea, God's strict justice was transformed to kindness, that is, left was transformed to right. The Jewish People merited "the revelation of the sparkling primal light of the World of Divine Unity, where all is one and no evil abounds" (Rav Kook, Orot HaTeshuvah 12:5).

This principle can also be applied to understand the mitzvah of obeying the verdicts of the Great Rabbinical Court and not rebelling against its words. "You must keep the Torah as they interpret it for you, and follow the laws that they legislate for you. Do not stray to the right or left from the word that they declare to you" (Deuteronomy 17:11). Rashi comments, "Even if they say to you that right is left or that left is right, but certainly if they tell you that right is right and that left is left." In other words, if the sages tell you that what seems to you to be divine kindness is really strict justice, and what seems to you to be strict justice is really kindness, you must heed them, for their perceptions and vision are profound, penetrating further than a superficial glance bereft of wisdom and understanding.

When approaching the political and social divide in modern Israel, we see how the community is splitting into right and left – yet that too is clearly on a superficial level, viewed from the outside. Whoever takes a deeper look to understand the entire marvelous process of the generation of rebirth, of the ingathering of the exiles, and the beginning of the raising of Israel's stature in their land, can understand that when "left" seemingly has the upper hand, when strict justice holds sway and God's countenance is concealed, within these very traits, and from their very midst emerges "right", kindness and goodness to Israel and to the entire world.

Each day when we recite the eternal song of the sea, and especially on the seventh day of Passover, the day the sea was split, we must appreciate how everything is turning out for the best – the mighty obstacles blocking our path can, with God's help, disappear in a moment, while strict justice and God's hiding His countenance from us conceal within them His kindness and benevolence.

The day is not far off when God will show us miracles like the time when we left Egypt. Then, all the earth's inhabitants will recognize and know that the God of Israel is King, and His sovereignty rules over all. "Then Moses and Israel [will] sing this song" – the song of faith and thanks that Israel sings in every generation, and in the future.

How fortunate we are and how good our lot that we are privileged to see the beginning of the fulfillment of the *Shira*, which states, "O bring them and plant them on the mount You possess. The place You dwell in is Your accomplishment, God. The shrine of God Your Hands have founded. God will reign forever and ever" (Exodus 15:17–18). Rashi comments, "The Temple will be built with two hands. And when will that occur? When God reigns forever and ever – in the future when all sovereignty is his.

How fortunate we are, how good our portion, that we are privileged to belong to the nation who proclaim God's Oneness. They are "believers and the sons of believers" (Shabbat 97a) that "the Lord is good to all; and His tender mercies are over all His works" (Psalms 145:9).

Chapter 12

The Omer: From Political Freedom to Spiritual Freedom

THE COUNTING OF THE OMER COMES BETWEEN TWO (flour) *Minchah* offerings; the barley offering brought on the second day of Pesach, and the wheat offering brought on Shavuot. Rabbi Abraham Isaac Kook explains that these two offerings hint to us about man's gradual spiritual improvement. That is, the Rabbis viewed barley as an animal food, alluding to man on an animal level, and they viewed wheat as a food for human beings, alluding to the highest spiritual level man has ever achieved, that of the Sinai Revelation.

When an infant is born, we ask how much he weighs. By the time he comes under the chupah, however, we have other questions. We want to know if he is a good person with good traits and good deeds. It is the same during the counting of the Omer. At the start of Pesach we are preoccupied with the Jews' material and physical survival, and at the end, when we get to Shavuot, we are more concerned with the spiritual level of the individual Jew and the Jewish People.

Our teachers explain beautifully the words we recite in our prayers, "Bring us to our land with heads held high [*komemiyut*]" (Blessings before the Shema.) *Komemiyut* (which appears in Leviticus 26:13) is a double form of *koma*, stage, hence we pray for redemption "in two stages [*komot*]" (Bava Batra 75a). In the first stage, we are occupied with the physical construction of a state, but we are advancing on to the next stage, involving the spiritual status of the nation, similar to the Revelation at Sinai.

In our day, we have begun to see the first stage through the ingathering of the exiles, and the establishment of the State of Israel. The second stage is the spiritual stage, the flourishing of the benevolent, illuminating soul of the Jewish People in the Land. Through achievement of this political and spiritual freedom together, with the People of Israel living in the Land of Israel, may we merit to see all mankind enjoying material plenty and spiritual light and everything that is good, as indeed God promised Abraham: "Go away from your land . . . to the land that I will show you. I will make you into a great nation. . . . You shall become a blessing. All the families of the earth shall be blessed through you" (Genesis 12:1–3).

LAG BA-OMER

Rabbi Shimon Bar Yochai Loves our People, Land and Torah.

The bonfires that the masses of our people light throughout Israel and the world on Lag Ba-omer are a sort of memorial candle for the noble spirit of Rabbi Shimon Bar Yochai, (aka Rashbi,) who ascended to the highest heavens on Lag Ba-omer. No personage in Jewish history has merited a memorial day in which the entire Jewish People takes part, from the entire social spectrum and from all streams of Judaism, observant and nonobservant, right wing and left, and in almost all communities. Not one of the patriarchs, Abraham, Isaac and Jacob, Moses, Aaron or King David, and not one of the illustrious rabbis of our people has ever merited that the entire nation should recall their name and make a *hilula*, a memorial celebration, on the anniversary of their passing.

How did Rashbi merit this great honor? Some say it is because he wrote the holy Zohar, which illuminates the souls of those who delve into Jewish mysticism and the secrets of the Jewish People. That is our inner wisdom, the *Kabbala*. Yet we must ask in turn how Rashbi was so privileged to have the holy Zohar revealed to him. Indeed, when we study and ponder the story of Rashbi's life, we discover that he displayed self-sacrifice on behalf of the People, Land and Torah of Israel, as our sages taught us:

> One time Rabbi Yehuda, Rabbi Yossi and Rashbi were seated together, and Yehuda ben Gerim was sitting with them. Said Rabbi Yehuda, "How fine the deeds of this nation [the Romans]! They installed marketplaces, bridges and bathhouses!" Rabbi Yossi remained silent. Rashbi responded, "They did nothing that didn't serve their own interests. They installed marketplaces to house harlots there; bathhouses so they could pamper themselves, and bridges as a means of collecting royal tolls." Yehuda ben Gerim went and reported their words to the Romans . . . (Shabbat 33b).

The results are well-known. Rashbi was persecuted and forced to flee with his son, and to hide in a cave for twelve years. His unwillingness to flatter the Romans and resign himself to their ruling over Eretz Yisrael stemmed from great love and faith in our People, Torah and Land. By such means he merited to discover many secrets of Jewish mysticism, recorded in the holy book of the Zohar.

Today as well, those who carry on the spirit of Rashbi and his mentor Rabbi Akiva, are the ones who truly love the People, Torah and Land of Israel. These Jews risk their lives for the glory of Israel and God, which is being revealed through Israel's rebirth in Eretz Yisrael. Indeed, the greatest kabbalists through all of the generations were lovers of Eretz Yisrael and came to live there.

These include Ramban, the Arizal, Ramchal, and the disciples of the Baal Shem Tov and of the Vilna Gaon.

In recent times we have seen that master of the light of Torah, Rabbi Avraham Yitzchak Kook, *zt"l*, together with his disciples and his disciple's disciples, totally devoted to settling Eretz Yisrael and learning the Torah of Eretz Yisrael. By doing so, they increase the Torah's light, the light of love and faith, and they carry on the path of Rashbi.

The day is not far off when through us will be fulfilled, "Bar Yochai! Fortunate are your forbears! Fortunate is the nation that learns from you, fortunate are those who dwell on your secret, enveloped in the breastplate of your *Urim VeTumim*."

THREE CROWNS

Rabbi Shimon bar Yochai says, "There are three crowns: the crown of Torah, of priesthood and of monarchy, and the crown of a good name surpasses them all" (Avot 4:14). Rashi explains, "Someone with a good name and good deeds is better than anyone else, as it says, 'A good name [i.e. reputation] is better than precious ointment' (Ecclesiastes 7:1)." Rabbi Shimon bar Yochai, with his "good name," was privileged to write the Zohar. That work is shedding more and more light through its sweet luminance, and it is by virtue of this luminance that we leave the exile (Zohar, Naso). How much more does it light our path when we are already rising to rebirth in our Holy Land which Rabbi Shimon bar Yochai loved so much, and for which he showed such self-sacrifice.

Rabbi Shimon bar Yochai was a disciple of Rabbi Akiva. The two of them, master and disciple, both felt the pain of the nation, which in those days was under Roman control. The Romans enacted decrees against the Jewish people, with the goal of humiliating them, subjugating them and weakening them, especially by their decree against Torah study. They knew that nothing so strengthens the Jewish people, giving them the fortitude to withstand the grave crisis following the destruction of the Temple, more than the study of our holy Torah.

Indeed, Rabbi Akiva would gather large crowds and teach Torah. He had no fear of the Romans. Ultimately, however, he was arrested, imprisoned and taken out to be cruelly executed. The Romans combed his flesh with iron combs. In his great love for God, he accepted upon himself the yoke of the kingdom of heaven, and his soul departed as he recited the Shema.

Rabbi Shimon bar Yochai followed in the path of his master, Rabbi Akiva (see Berachot 61b) and he spoke negatively against the Romans, despite the danger. Ultimately he was compelled to flee from them and to hide for twelve years in a cave, together with his son. Neither Rabbi Akiva nor Rabbi Shimon bar Yochai could bear the humiliation of the Jewish People – the nation that God chose from all others – and they put themselves at risk for the glory of their people.

Today, after thousands of years of exile in which the glory of Israel was trampled to the dust, how fortunate we are that we are returning to our land, and that the glory of the Jewish people is being reinstated. The Torah is returning to its abode. The decrees of the Romans and of all of Israel's enemies through the exile, to prevent Jews from learning Torah, did not succeed. The self-sacrifice of Rabbi Akiva and of all the Jews over Torah learning did not go to waste. Today, thank God, the State of Israel is the world center of Torah learning. We are witnessing the great thirst of our nation to learn about the light of Rabbi Shimon bar Yochai, which is increasing from day to day, echoing the plea of the sweet singer of Israel, King David: "Open my eyes that I may behold wondrous things from Your Torah" (Psalm 119:18). That light is hastening our own redemption and the redemption of the world.

Chapter 13
Memorial Day for the Fallen Soldiers of Israel and Victims of Terror

"BE STRONG AND OF GOOD COURAGE" (JOSHUA 1:6–7:9) – THEN AND NOW

God says "Be strong and of good courage" to Joshua three times: "Be strong and of good courage, for you shall cause this people to inherit the land which I swore to their fathers to give them. Be but strong and of good courage, and keep all the Torah which Moses My servant commanded you. . . . Have I not commanded you, 'Be strong and of good courage, be neither afraid nor dismayed?'" (Joshua 1:6–7,9).

Rashi comments: The first occurrence of this expression calls upon Joshua to tend to Israel's material needs, the second calls upon him to study Torah and to teach it to the Jewish People, and the third calls upon him to be courageous and not to fear battle.

Indeed, three main tasks faced the generation of Joshua. The first was to support themselves materially by means of physical labor and a healthy economy, since the manna had ceased to fall from heaven. The second was to strengthen public Torah learning since Moses, their spiritual and political leader, had passed away.

The third was to go to war and to conquer the Land and defend it against Israel's enemies.

These three tasks demand "strength" and "courage." Rabbi Elijah of Vilna comments that these two words refer to "physical strength and spiritual courage," since these do not come easily, but through effort, exertion and constant strengthening of one's self.

Yet of the three subjects mentioned above, only the third was explicitly stated to Joshua as a command: "Have I not commanded you. . . ." Perhaps regarding war and battle, strength and courage are preconditions to victory, hence not mere encouragement but requisite fortitude.

Our current challenges resemble that of Joshua's generation.

Just as then the Jews were arriving after hundreds of years of exile in Egypt, so too are we gathering together in our land following two thousand years of exile. Following the Egyptian exile, the Jews had to develop a healthy, organized economy after forty years in which they ate food from heaven. We too are creating a modern state in a new global environment and have to develop our economy to be independent and healthy.

In Joshua's generation part of the Torah was forgotten due to the death of Moses, and Joshua had to strengthen Torah learning among the people. In our own generation, especially since the "enlightenment" movement in Europe, many Jews have succumbed to foreign influences and fallen away from their Jewish identity and culture. We have to strengthen our identity as Jews and strengthen our spirits, mainly through increasing Torah learning in all avenues possible.

Joshua's generation fought to conquer and take hold of the Land, and similarly today our army, the IDF, is needed to fight for the continued survival of our state's existence.

So we must take heed, just as God specifically commanded Joshua not to fear the tribulations of war, but rather gather more "strength and courage" for the task. We are especially commanded not to fear the war threats of our enemies. Quite the contrary, we must strengthen ourselves militarily and, to no less of an extent, we must develop our personal and national courage to win the spiritual battle for the eternal soul of our nation.

Our victory, in body and spirit, will grant merit to the holy soldiers and victims of terror who showed us the way to have "strength and courage" in our continued redemption, until we soon see the complete return of our people to our land and to our eternal heritage. Amen.

Chapter 14

Israel Independence Day: "In the Multitude is the King's Glory"

EZEKIEL 36 DESCRIBES THE GRADUAL PROCESS OF ISRAEL's redemption. The first stage is the ingathering of the exiles, as it says, "I will take you from among the nations, and gather you out of all the countries, and will bring you into your own land" (verse 24). Our sages as well (Sanhedrin 98a), in their answer to the question about what is the sign of the end of exile, point to the ingathering of the exiles and the flowering of the Land:

"Rabbi Abba said: You have no greater sign of the revealed end of days than this, as it says, 'But you, O mountains of Israel, shall shoot forth your branches and yield your fruit to My people Israel; for they are at hand to come'" (Ezekiel 36:8).

After the ingathering of the exiles and the flowering of the Land, as in our own day, will come a stage of national purification, and that, too, will come in stages: "I will sprinkle clean water upon you, and you shall be clean. From all your uncleanness and from all your idols will I cleanse you" (36:25). We shall be cleansed of all those influences of the exile that clung to us when we were amongst the nations, and which led to assimilation, weakness and divisiveness, controversy and groundless hatred. Israel in the exile is likened to a precious jewel that has been sullied in dirt and mud. In Eretz Yisrael we shall be purified by a return to our Torah and to Jewish tradition.

The next stage of spiritual improvement shall be: "A new heart also will I give you, and a new spirit will I put within you. I will take away the stony heart out of your flesh, and I will give you a heart of flesh" (verse 26). The new heart and spirit will replace our hearts of stone that have no sensitivity to our fellow man, and sometimes no feeling at all, with a feeling, sensitive heart, a good heart, that will have an influence on the lives of the individual, the family and the entire nation.

Regarding the third stage it says, "I will put My spirit within you, and cause you to walk in My statutes, and you shall keep My ordinances and do them" (verse 27). In other words, we will keep the Torah and its mitzvot, and we shall be the living fulfillment of God's words:

> You shall dwell in the land that I gave to your fathers; and you shall be My people, and I will be your God. . . . I will cause the cities to be inhabited, and the waste places shall be built. The land that was desolate shall be tilled. . . . Then the nations that are left round about you shall know that I, the Lord have built the ruined places, and planted that which was desolate; I the Lord have spoken it, and I will do it (verses 36:28,33,36).

In those days, the Jewish People, settled in their land, shall experience enormous natural growth, as it says:

> Thus says the Lord God: I will yet for this be inquired of by the house of Israel, to do it for them. I will multiply them, the men, like a flock. . . . The waste cities shall be filled with flocks of men; and they shall know that I am the Lord (verse 37).

Today, as we set out to celebrate over seventy years to the State of Israel, we must ponder and observe with our own eyes the reality in which we live, through the vision of the prophets of Israel, and the vision of Ezekiel specifically. How fortunate we are to be at the height of the ingathering of the exiles – millions of Jews are already living in the Land, and, God willing, millions more will come home. The land is flowering and developing in gigantic strides, economically, in terms of infrastructure and the building of cities and towns. All of this is preparation for the next stage: investing spiritual content into our national home, which will come about gradually, giving us a "a new heart and a new spirit," referring to the great repentance that will characterize the coming generations.

The first buds of this process are already discernable in our own generation, by way of the awakening of interest and respect for the Torah and for Jewish tradition. This thirst will increase as we advance upward on the path to complete redemption. The return to Torah and to faith will also bring about a change in the demographic situation in Israel. The Jewish People will increase, as we are witnessing today, especially in religious families. Those families cut off in the Holocaust will be privileged to see how they will increase remarkably. Indeed, families of survivors that have dozens of grandchildren and great-grandchildren are already not a rare sight in our streets.

Six-hundred-thousand Jews left Egypt and with six-hundred-thousand we established the State of Israel. Already we merit to have over six-million Jews in Israel. Soon this number will constitute a majority of the Jews living today, and "in the multitude of the people is the King's glory" (Proverbs 14:28).

The more the Jews proliferate in Israel, the more it will be revealed for all to see that Hashem, the God of Israel, is King, and His Kingdom rules over all. By such means, "all the inhabitants of the earth will recognize and know that every knee will prostrate itself before You and every tongue will swear before You . . . All will undertake the yoke of Your Kingdom, and You shall reign over them forever and ever. . . . As it says, 'The Lord shall be King over all the earth. On that day shall He be one and His name one'" (Aleinu).

"MAY OUR EYES SEE YOUR RETURN IN MERCY TO ZION."

In 1956, Rav Tzvi Yehuda HaKohen Kook said:

"We must be very joyous on Independence Day. We must be joyous over the revelation of the Divine Presence, the return to Zion, and the rebirth of the Jewish People. All the rebuilding, rebirth and survival of the State of Israel is interwoven with great miracles that God has shown us. . . . Fifty years ago who could have imagined that the Turks, who ruled triumphantly over our land, would be entirely ousted? Ten years ago, would anyone have thought that mighty England would be forced to give up its rule over our country? Every tractor and tank and plane defending our country has divine holiness. Every aspect and every detail is a revelation of the divine, national content of the holiness of Israel. Even if many lack this awareness that it is Divine Providence which guides what is occurring, that is the reality. It is solid fact that will not go away, whether or not people recognize it. . . .

"True, the entire land has not yet been conquered – even Jerusalem, the sanctuary of our kingdom is not yet entirely in our hands [This was eleven years before the Six Day War]. In both quality and quantity, our rule over the Land must be completed and developed. Yet the State's establishment constitutes the revelation of the Divine Kingdom, and we must be exceedingly joyful on Yom HaAtzma'ut over having merited to become an independent country. . . ." (Sichot HaRav Tzvi Yehuda Kook, on the 5th Israel Independence Day).

If some seventy years ago, when the State of Israel was at the start of its path, we were required to rejoice over the kindness God performed for us in establishing a State, all the more so now when over six-million Jews live here. Israel is making enormous strides. It is becoming one of the strongest countries militarily and economically. We see clearly how the words, "May our eyes see [*tirena*] Your kingdom" [from the *kedusha* prayer] are being fulfilled – through our tangible nation state. The day is not far off when we will all merit the fulfillment of the entreaty, "May our eyes see [*ve'techezena*] Your return in mercy to Zion," [from the Amida prayer] not just the restoration of the kingdom, but the restoration of the soul to the Temple sanctuary. We have merited *tirena*, referring to external vision. Now our eyes are raised to God in hopes of *techezena*, a more spiritual vision. (ibid, Rav Tzvi Yehuda Kook).

FROM POLITICAL TO SPIRITUAL INDEPENDENCE

The political independence which we merited in 1948 was the preface to Israel's developing a national character. As is known, there are two main stages in the rebirth of the Jewish People in their land, as alluded to in the blessings preceding the Shema prayer: (1) "Break the yoke from our necks and (2) make us go upright to our land." The first stage consists of the physical rebirth of the nation. After two thousand years of exile, during which time we were compared to dry bones (Ezekiel 37), we are now privileged to live as a free people in our land. The second stage consists of the rebirth of the soul of the Jewish People – Israel's reappearance as a unique spiritual entity, "a nation created by God to tell His praise" (Isaiah 43:21).

Just as the transition from exile to political independence involved enormous difficulties, struggles and wars until we merited a state of our own, so does the transition from political to spiritual independence naturally involve internal and external difficulties and struggles. With every transition that one undergoes, one must be very patient until matters ultimately become clarified. Whether the issue is the move from childhood to adulthood or from adulthood to old age, there is a clarification process fraught with hardships and crises.

Frequently we find ourselves in fierce election campaigns in which some of the parties and candidates for national leadership are struggling to attain the reins of power with the intent of influencing the spiritual fabric of the State of Israel. These struggles are a concrete expression of the transition process from political independence to clarification of the identity, common ground and purpose of the Jewish People as they ascend on the path towards salvation and complete redemption. We must struggle to advance, and at the same time, arm ourselves with patience and faith, until God's promise is fulfilled: "You will be a kingdom of priests and a holy nation to Me" (Exodus 19:6).

THE STATE OF ISRAEL, FOUNDATION OF GOD'S THRONE ON EARTH

A hundred years ago, Rabbi Avraham Yitzchak Kook, *zt"l* wrote about the difference between the State of Israel (which at the time was still just a vision) and the rest of the nations of the world:

"A normal country is like a large insurance company. It is not the source of its citizen's supreme joy. Ideals, which are the crowning glory of mankind, hover above a country and do not touch it. Not so a country founded on ideals and inherently based on the loftiest message. Such countries truly constitute their citizen's greatest joy. Therefore, the State of Israel is truly the most supreme on the scale of joy, and it constitutes the foundation of God's throne on earth. Its entire purpose is that God should be one and His name one, truly the greatest source of joy" (see Orot 160).

We conclude our daily prayers with the words, "The Lord shall be King over all the earth. On that day shall the Lord be One and His name one" (Zechariah 14:9). In the future, people will be so happy that even in response to strict divine justice for which we presently recite, "Blessed is the Judge of Truth" (as we do today upon bad tidings of a death), they will recite, "Blessed is He who is good and benevolent", which is presently recited only upon good tidings. (See Pesachim 50a). All this will come to pass when the State of Israel appears and is revealed in all its greatness and glory.

To many, Rav Kook's vision of the State of Israel that will serve as a light to the nations, seems to be crumbling before our eyes, as we witness spiritual and moral deterioration occurring among some of our leaders who speak of plans to cut off portions of our homeland. On the birthday of our beloved country, while we rejoice over the millions of Jews who are being gathered in from the world over, and the enormous economic development – we ask ourselves, seeing the nadir to which we have fallen: Shall we ever emerge from the moral and spiritual crisis visiting our country?

Rav Kook taught with full certainty that all this is a descent for the sake of ascent:

"All those building up the nation will arrive at the depths of this truth, that our nation will be built and consolidated, and will be restored to its strength, to all the foundations of its life by way of its faith and its fear of God, its hallowed noble content spreading and becoming stronger and more developed. Then, with a voice full of valor and might they will proclaim with a loud cry, 'Come, let us return to God!'" (Orot HaTeshuvah 15:11).

The present crisis will quickly lead to a great movement of return to ourselves, our Torah, our roots, our Father in Heaven. Through this, we will merit to see not only the physical building of our country, but also the revealed benevolent soul of our nation which will shine on the entire world. As Rav Kook said, "The State of Israel is the foundation of God's throne on earth" and as the prophets of Israel said, "For out of Zion shall go forth the Torah, and the word of God from Jerusalem" (Isaiah 2:4). Speedily in our day. Amen.

Chapter 15

Jerusalem Day: Jerusalem – Heart of the Universe

Throughout the generations, the Jewish People have prayed three times a day, entreating God to rebuild Jerusalem: "To Jerusalem, Your city, return in mercy, and dwell therein as You have spoken. Rebuild it soon in our days as an eternal edifice." (Shemoneh Esreh).

Whenever a Jew recites the Grace after Meals, he mentions the rebuilding of Jerusalem: "Rebuild Jerusalem, the Holy City, soon in our day." A Jewish bridegroom, at the most important moment of his life, proclaims, "If I forget you, O Jerusalem, let my right hand lose its cunning" (Psalms 137:5).

The Torah views the rebuilding of Jerusalem as a supreme, holy value that we must never forget. Quite the contrary, we must cling to it not only in our prayers and blessings, but tangibly as well, through actually settling and rebuilding Jerusalem.

Jerusalem is compared to the heart of the Jewish People and the heart of the world. This place was chosen by God as the central place in the world for God's glory and kingdom to be revealed. It is from here that God's word goes out to the entire world, as the prophet said, "For out of Zion shall go forth the law, and the word of God from Jerusalem" (Isaiah 2:3). The only precondition for the Jewish People's fulfilling their universal task of bringing light to the world, is the reconstruction of earthly Jerusalem and its being under Jewish control. Through this, celestial Jerusalem will also be rebuilt, showering light and consummate goodness upon the whole world.

Just as the soul can be revealed only through the body, the soul of our nation and the light of the Jewish People can be revealed only when we are inhabiting Jerusalem, rebuilt in all its glory. Our sages said, "Jerusalem is the light of the universe," yet this is so only when Israel shall rebuild it and dwell in it.

This insight can help us comprehend the determined opposition of all those persons and groups that do not desire the rebuilding of Jerusalem, because they do not desire the light of the universe. There are those for whom heretical darkness of the spirit is convenient. There are those on earth who find their sustenance in darkness and night. "You make darkness, and it is night, when all the beasts of the forest do creep forth. The young lions roar after their prey" (Psalms 104:20–21).

Let us not be overwhelmed by the opposition of the nations to the rebuilding of Jerusalem. Let us neither be overwhelmed by opposition from within, which stems from spiritual weakness and lack of faith. Those forces do not understand the meaning of the light of the universe being revealed through Jerusalem's reconstruction. They cannot fathom that every Jewish home in Jerusalem adds light to the whole house of Israel, and to all of mankind. "He who sits in the heavens laughs. The Lord has them in derision" (Psalms 2:4). God laughs at all those who say of Jerusalem, "Raze it! Raze it! To its very foundations" (Psalm 137:7).

We have a tradition from our prophets and sages that when the Jewish People arise to rebirth in Eretz Yisrael, the nations will fight us with the goal of snuffing out "the candle of the world" and of Jerusalem, as it says, "Why are the nations in an uproar?

And why do the peoples mutter in vain? The kings of the earth join ranks. The rulers take counsel together against the Lord and against His anointed" (Psalm 2:1–2). The threat comes not just from without, however, but from within as well. Jews of weak faith, who do not know or understand the national and universal significance of Jewish sovereignty over Jerusalem, will rise up, and they will talk about partitioning Jerusalem and handing it over to foreign nations. They will not understand that allowing the nations control over Jerusalem, or even over part of it, means darkness for the world.

Yet the day is not far off when God's promise to Israel and to the entire world will be fulfilled: Israel will return to Jerusalem and bring light and goodness to the world. Then we will be living fulfillment of Isaiah 66:13: "As one whom his mother comforts, so will I comfort you; and you shall be comforted in Jerusalem."

RAISE "THE FLAG OF JERUSALEM" ON JERUSALEM DAY

Over a hundred years ago, Rabbi Avraham Yitzchak HaKohen Kook called for the establishment of a political movement by the name of "Degel Yerushalayim," whose purpose would be to infuse holiness into the course of the national rebirth which was then in its beginnings. Rav Kook had seen how the Zionist Movement was being run in accordance with an ideology founded on secularism. Rav Kook saw in this a major deterrence to the process of rebirth of the Jewish People in the Land of Israel.

Three main goals stood before him in the establishment of Degel Yerushalayim:

1. A quantitative goal: To unite the religious and Chareidi publics – who had not joined the Zionist Movement due to its distance from religion and Jewishness – into an influential political body that would be a partner in the process of rebirth.

Had this process succeeded, it would have brought about a great wave of Aliyah amongst the Chareidi public in advance of the Holocaust, and would have influenced the Jewish image of the State-in-the-Making, and of the State of Israel today.

2. A qualitative goal: To breath a holy fire into the onset of the process of rebirth. Already back then, Zionism was lacking the dimension of holiness, and it viewed religion as a private matter and not a national matter at all. Had Rav Kook succeeded, the worldview that separates church and state would never have gained political and public relevance.

3. To bring the Jewish People and the world to recognize that the rebirth of the Jewish People in their land is a matter of importance for the whole world, just as all the prophets of Israel prophesied. Israel is the light of the world. Israel's recognizing their identity, uniqueness and destiny would breathe a great spirit into them, and would give them the strength and ability to withstand the pressures of the nations, knowing why they had arisen to rebirth and established a state.

"If I forget you, O Jerusalem, let my right hand lose its cunning" (Psalm 137:5).

On this Jerusalem Day, let us remember that Jerusalem is the holy city, the city in which holiness is revealed on earth. And in order that holiness be revealed, we must return to Rav Kook's plan to "raise up the flag of Jerusalem," i.e., to establish a socio-political-religious movement that will infuse holy content into the entire process of national rebirth. And may we thereby merit to see with our own eyes how the words of the prophet will be revealed: For out of Zion shall go forth the Torah, and the word of the Lord from Jerusalem" (Isaiah 2:4).

"RETURN IN MERCY TO YOUR CITY, JERUSALEM."

From the 5th of Iyar, Israel's Independence Day, we ascend in holiness to the 28th of Iyar, Jerusalem Day. And from "With love You led the people You redeemed" (Exodus 15:13), we arrive at the higher spiritual level of "With might, You led them to Your holy shrine" (ibid.) – Jerusalem, site of our Temple.

Jerusalem is the heart of Eretz Yisrael, the center of its life, and it is linked to all of Eretz Yisrael. Rabbi Tzvi Yehuda Kook, *zt"l*, who merited to be among the first to arrive at the Western Wall on the day of its liberation, was requested on that historic occasion to make a radio address, addressing a few words to the world. In his confident, roaring voice, he proclaimed: "Let it henceforth be known to the entire Jewish People, to the entire world and all who inhabit it once and for all, that on orders from the Creator of the universe, on orders of Him who knows all human history in advance, we have arrived and returned home, and we will never leave here!"

Rabbi Tzvi Yehuda Kook *zt"l*, with his deep and penetrating vision, foresaw the opposition – from within and from without – that would arise against Israel's returning to the Kotel and the Temple Mount, and his cry has echoed from then until today.

Today, the war over Jerusalem has not ended. Our enemies have not resigned themselves to Jewish rule over Jerusalem, and they continue to fight us, with their struggle always taking different forms. Sometimes, it involves an all-out war, like the Yom Kippur war. Sometimes it involves an intifada, and sometimes, they stealthily employ a "peace attack," like the wretched Oslo Accords, whose purpose was the destruction of the State of Israel.

Our enemy's goal is to snuff out the light of the Jewish people in Eretz Yisrael, and in Jerusalem specifically. The Rabbis said, "Jerusalem is the light of the universe," and the war over Jerusalem is not just a physical war, but, first and foremost, a war over the revelation of God's light in the world. Whoever settles in Jerusalem, building it and defending it, increases light and goodness in the world. The Jewish people and our political and military leadership need and have an obligation to learn what Jerusalem is, and what value it has for the Jewish people and for the entire world. Moreover, they must learn to comprehend the essence of Jerusalem's soul. By such means, they will draw the strength and fortitude required to face up to the struggles and battles over Israel and over Jerusalem. On Jerusalem Day, we must learn and delve deeply into its meaning. We must recognize and connect ourselves to it, and we must ascend to Jerusalem and to rejoice in its happiness. May we be the living fulfillment of the prayer: "Return in mercy to Your city Jerusalem, and dwell in it as You have promised" (Shemoneh Esreh).

"IF I FORGET YOU, O JERUSALEM, LET MY RIGHT HAND LOSE ITS CUNNING."

Every groom under the wedding canopy declares loyalty to Jerusalem, reciting the words, "If I forget you, O Jerusalem, let my right hand lose its cunning. Let my tongue cleave to the roof of my mouth if I do not remember you, if I do not set Jerusalem above my highest joy" (Psalms 137:5–6). For thousands of years, millions of Jews have poured forth tears like water with their prayer, "Return, in mercy, to Your city, Jerusalem. Dwell within it as You said You would" (Shemoneh Esreh).

Whenever a Jew eats bread, he recalls Jerusalem and the longing for its rebuilding with the words, "Rebuild Jerusalem the holy city speedily in our day" (Grace after Meals). All such prayers and customs which have accompanied us for thousands of years have the purpose of strengthening our spiritual and material connection to Jerusalem, heart of the nation. Only in rebuilt Jerusalem will the Jewish nation be revealed in its full glory and might through the Torah, prophecy, the Temple and monarchy. Only through our people's return to Jerusalem, and our control over Jerusalem, are we able to increase light and goodness in the world, for Jerusalem is the light of the world.

Right now, the remarkable sight of the return to Zion and the rebuilding of Jerusalem is bringing the hope to hundreds of millions of people that the world will be illuminated by the Jewish People with the light of faith, the light of love, the light of joy. As we say in our morning prayers, "May a new light shine over Zion." Moreover, Isaiah said (2:3), "Many people shall go and say, 'Come! Let us go up to the mountain of the Lord, to the house of the God of Jacob. He will teach us of His ways, and we will walk in His paths.' For out of Zion shall go forth Torah, and the word of the Lord from Jerusalem." The divine promise to Abraham will then be fulfilled, "I will make you into a great nation. . . . All the families of the earth will be blessed through you" (Genesis 12:2, 3).

It is true that in face of the "dreamlike return of Zion's captivity" (Psalm 126:1), forces of darkness are rising up that cannot bear the light emerging from Zion and Jerusalem, just as a bat cannot bear the light of day. They are fighting to dispossess us of Jerusalem and to destroy it, saying, "Raze it! Raze it! To its very foundations" (Psalm 137:7).

Yet, "He who sits in heavens laughs. The Lord mocks them. . . . You shall break them with a rod of iron. You shall dash them to pieces like a potter's vessel" (Psalms 2:9). "For the Lord will not cast off His people, nor will He forsake His inheritance" (Psalms 94:14); "As the mountains are round about Jerusalem, so the Lord is round about His people henceforth and forever" (Psalm 125:2).

Chapter 16

Shavuot: Festival of the Giving of the Torah

THE TORAH WAS GIVEN TO THE JEWISH PEOPLE, AND NOT to this individual or that, neither to any particular party or stream within the Jewish People. Only when Israel was united as one man with one heart did they receive the Torah at Sinai. Before the Sinai Revelation, the Jewish people repented, abandoning their divisiveness and uniting, as it says, "They had departed from Rephidim and had arrived in the Sinai Desert, camping in the wilderness. Israel camped opposite the mountain" (Exodus 19:2). Rashi comments, "As one man, with one heart." From the receiving of the Torah, some 3000 years ago, until today, the Jewish people have never ceased to learn, teach, and fulfill our holy Torah. The Torah is a book of life. As it says, "It is a tree of life for those who take hold of it" (Proverbs 3:18).

The knowledge that the Torah was imparted to the entire Jewish People is bequeathed to every Jewish child when he is learning to talk. His father then teaches him, "Moses prescribed the Torah to us, an eternal heritage to the congregation of Jacob" (Deuteronomy 33:4; Rambam, Hilchot Talmud Torah 1:6). Our holy Torah is a heritage for the entire Jewish People.

Likewise each day, before we learn Torah, we bless God, "who chose us from amongst all nations and gave us His Torah." The blessing refers to us in the plural. Every approach to Torah learning must start with an awareness that God chose us from amongst all the nations, that the Jewish People are a chosen people, a "kingdom of priests and a holy people" (see Exodus 19:5–6). Torah learning that does not begin with recitation of the Torah blessing to God "who chose us from amongst all nations," is what brought the exile upon us. As our sages say, "Why was the Land lost? Because they did not recite the blessings before Torah learning" (see Bava Metzia 85, Sichot HaRav Tzvi Yehuda Kook, Talmud Torah 2).

Today, how fortunate we are and how pleasant our lot that after two thousand years of exile we have finally merited to return to our land. And we are not only returning to our land, but to ourselves and to our Torah, our heritage. Here in Eretz Yisrael, the special soul of the Jewish People as a chosen people, a kingdom of priests and a holy nation, is increasingly being revealed for all to see. True, we are still only at the start of the process of rebirth, and there is still enormous confusion and lack of knowledge and understanding regarding the essence, identity and purpose of our people, chosen by God to bring light to the world. Yet we can already see the light at the end of the tunnel, in the form of tens of thousands of our Jewish brethren who are returning to our holy Torah, filling the synagogues and study halls, and reciting the Torah blessing, praising God "who chose us from amongst all nations and gave us His Torah." On Shavuot, we recite with enormous joy, "You chose us from amongst all peoples. You loved us and wanted us . . . and You lovingly gave us holidays for joy, festivals and good times for rejoicing, including this Shavuot holiday, the festival of the giving of the Torah."

Today, our generation, the generation of the rebirth and of ingathering of the exiles, is facing spiritual, social and political crises. The means of rectifying this complex situation is to foment a change in culture and education, and to establish Torah learning as a national value of the first order. All Jewish children, and adults as well, should be learning Torah, as was the situation during the time of King Hezekiah, who passed a compulsory education law. If during the dark exile, Torah learning illuminated the Jewish souls, ensuring their survival, all the more so in the Land of Israel and the State of Israel, that the Torah learning of myriad Jews should strengthen the spirit of the nation.

Our holy Torah belongs to the entire Jewish people, and to every individual Jew. We shall certainly be the living fulfillment of the blessing, "Our Father! Merciful Father! You, who are ever compassionate! Have pity on us and inspire us to understand and discern, to perceive, learn and teach, to observe, do and fulfill gladly all the teachings of Your Torah" (Blessings of the Shema).

"MY SPIRIT . . . AND MY WORDS . . . SHALL NOT DEPART FROM YOUR MOUTH NOR FROM THE MOUTH OF YOUR CHILDREN."

At the Sinai Revelation, "Moses led the people out of the camp toward the divine presence. They stood transfixed at the foot of the mountain" (Exodus 19:17). Rashi comments, "The mountain was torn from its place and overturned upon them like a basin. God said, 'if you accept the Torah, fine. Otherwise, this shall be your burial place" (Shabbat 88a). And why did God overturn the mountain upon them in this way? To make known the Torah's virtue, that Israel cannot survive without it. Had Israel accepted the Torah willingly, they would say that it is not essential and they can get along without it. After all, they received it of their own free will and they could have rejected it just as well. God therefore overturned the mountain upon them, to show that Israel cannot survive without the Torah, just as the world cannot exist without the Torah (see Maharal, Gur Arye).

Likewise, Scripture says of King Hezekiah, who was a penitent, "He drove a sword into the door of the study hall and he said, 'Whoever does not study Torah shall be impaled with this sword.' An examination was made from Dan to Beersheva and not a single ignoramus was found. . . . No one, child or adult, was found to be unfamiliar with Jewish law. . . ." (Sanhedrin 94b).

Rav Kook had a vision of "our nation being rebuilt and consolidated, regaining its strength and resuming all aspects of its life as a nation." This, he said, would occur "by way of their faith and reverence, their divine, hallowed, noble content spreading, gaining control, developing and becoming strong. All the nation's builders will arrive at the profound truth of this point" (Orot HeTeshuvah 15:11). How will the nation return to its spiritual nature? "Through mass Torah learning, through schools who will raise up Torah scholars and other schools where the masses can learn Torah on a regular basis."

Today, in the Jewish People's process of rebirth, we distinguish two stages. The first is the ingathering of the exiles and the establishment of a Jewish state, with economic and military might. The second stage is spiritual rebirth, fulfillment of the prophetic promise, "I will sprinkle clean water upon you. . . . A new heart also will I give you, and a new spirit will I put within you" (Ezekiel 36:25–6). This refers to the renewal of prophecy in Israel, as Rav Kook wrote:

> The great repentance that will revive the nation, and that will bring redemption to Israel and to the world, will be repentance that derives from the *ruach hakodesh* [prophetic intuition] that abounds amongst them" (ibid, 97).

What will lead to this spiritual renewal and rebirth? Torah learning.

The day is not far off when Israel, willingly and agreeably, will enact a Compulsory Torah Education Law. Then all Jewish children will learn Torah, which is the heritage of the entire Jewish

People, just as it was given at Sinai to all of Israel. Then, with our own eyes we will see the fulfillment of the divine promise, "This is My covenant with them – says the Lord: 'My spirit shall be upon you and My words which I have put in your mouth shall not depart from your mouth, nor from the mouth of your children, nor from the mouth of your children's children' – says the Lord – 'henceforth and forever'" (Isaiah 59:20–21).

THE JEWISH PEOPLE – AS ONE MAN AND OF ONE MIND

It says, "Israel camped opposite the mountain" (Exodus 19:2). Rashi explains, "As one man and of one mind, but all their other encampments were made in a spirit of resentment and dissension." The precondition for Israel's being ready for the Sinai Revelation was being as one man and of one mind, without resentment or dissension.

We can derive a lesson from a precise analysis of Rashi's wording: "As one man." Every individual has numerous limbs and organs and diverse attributes. Yet they all add up to one person, with each limb and organ and every attribute supplementing what is lacking in the others. It is the same with the Jewish People. Every Jew is different, "for neither in mind or appearance do they resemble one another" (Berachot 58). All the same, we are one people marching through history to our divine destiny, to serve as a light unto the nations.

Why was it necessary for Rashi to add "and of one mind"? Rashi was hinting that it is not enough that the Jewish people possess one "body," one national framework. That national framework needs a heart, a human heart, a center in which the whole Jewish People can be united and draw strength. Indeed, from time immemorial the Jewish People have always had one center, one heart. In the Desert, the *Mishkan* (tabernacle) was that heart, and in the Land, it was the First and Second Temples. They were the source from which the nation drew its psychological and spiritual strength. When we went into exile for two thousand years, the synagogues and study houses constituted a miniature Temple, and from them the nation drew strength to survive the darkness of exile.

Today, the Jewish People are in the midst of the ingathering of the exiles. Moreover, their renewed political entity is taking shape after two thousand years of exile, during which we were "one nation, scattered and divided" (Esther 3:8). At this time, we need not just external, physical unity, but even more so, and especially, internal unity, the unity of having one heart which can cause spiritual blood to flow to all parts of the nation. We need an exclusively Jewish culture, a culture based on and deriving nourishment from our holy Torah and eternal Jewish values. At the same time, that culture must be connected to the rebirth of our people in its land, as well as to the world that is progressively developing scientifically and technologically.

Just as the roots and trunk unite the branches of a tree, so too our traditions and Jewish roots will unite our people in its land. The great political change that has taken place calls for a change in attitude, such that school children of the whole nation will be educated, with love and faith, towards real Judaism. Through this, we will march upward together on the path to complete redemption.

Now, on our return to our land and to Jerusalem our capital, on the way to building the Third Temple – may it be soon in our day – the centrality of the State of Israel for the Jewish People and for all of mankind is being revealed more and more. Eretz Yisrael and Jerusalem are becoming the center of Torah on earth, leading to fulfillment of Isaiah's words: "For out of Zion shall go forth the Torah, and the word of the Lord from Jerusalem" (Isaiah 2:3).

Right now, despite all of the political struggles, we must remember and imbue in our hearts that when all is said and done, we are one nation – as one man, of one mind – whose purpose is to publicize that the Lord God of Israel is One and His kingdom rules over all.

FROM LOT, VIA RUTH, TO DAVID THE ANOINTED

King David was a descendant of Ruth the Moabite. "Moab" (lit., "from-father") received that name due to the shameful deed of Lot's daughter, who cohabited with her father while he was drunk, and thus bore Moab. She not only did this deed, but she immortalized this terrible act by calling her son "Moab."

All the same, from Moab emerged Ruth, who converted and entered under the wings of the Divine Presence. From her emerged King David, from whom the Messiah will be descended.

From here we learn that we must not mock or disdain any human being, even the most lowly. An example of such a person is Lot, a drunkard who became the symbol of a man who loses his Divine image during his drunkenness. We thus use the expression "Drunk as Lot" to describe those drunkards who have lost their Divine image.

We must learn from the stories of Ruth the Moabite, and from the chain of events leading from Lot to the Messiah, that we must not mock or dismiss any human being, even when he falls down low. We ask, "Who is like the Lord our God, enthroned on high?" (Psalm 113:5). At the same time, however, we believe that the same God who is "enthroned on high," also "looks far down to behold the things that are in heaven and earth" (Ibid. v. 6). He also "raises up the poor out of the dust and lifts the needy out of the ashes" (v. 7).

FAITHFUL SHEPHERDS

On Shavuot we encounter the two faithful shepherds of Israel, from Israel's beginnings and from the end of days. We encounter Moses, who led God's "flock" (Psalm 100:3) from when they were just starting out in Egypt and the desert, up until they reached the threshold of Eretz Yisrael. We also encounter King David, who led Israel in the heart of the Land and Jerusalem, and who will continue to lead when the Messianic King arrives and bestows his pure spirit upon the whole world: "For out of Zion shall go forth the Torah, and the word of the Lord from Jerusalem" (Isaiah 2:3).

The two great rulers of the Jewish People were each shepherds when they started out: "Moses tended the sheep of his father-in-law Jethro, sheik of Midian. He led the flock to the edge of the desert" (Exodus 3:1). Regarding King David as well, we find, "David said to Saul, 'Your servant kept his father's sheep'" (I Samuel 17:34). It is well known how faithful and devoted a shepherd was Moses. When he discerned that a young goat was missing, he went out to look for him until he found him and returned him. He supervised every small detail involving his flock. When David set out to persuade Saul that he could beat Goliath, he told him how he had killed the lion and the bear when they were coming to attack sheep from his flock, and he concluded, "This uncircumcised Philistine shall be as one of them" (I Samuel 17:36).

Moses, the shepherd and leader of the Jewish People as they were starting out, devoted himself, body and soul, to the Jewish People as a group and as individuals, starting in Egypt. King David, for his part, led the Jewish People in Eretz Yisrael, when they were being attacked by cruel enemies who went to war against Israel "in order to "taunt the armies of the Living God" (I Samuel 17:26). King David was revealed to be a strong, courageous fighter who smote and subjugated the enemies of Israel just as he had done to the lion and the bear. Simultaneously he was a holy man who employed his *ruach hakodesh*, his holy spirit, to write the Psalms.

These two leaders overcame internal crises and defeated external enemies out of their faith in the Eternal One of Israel, the uniqueness of the Jewish People and Israel's destiny as "a kingdom of priests and a holy nation" (Exodus 19:6). This faith gave them the strength, courage and determination to withstand all of the difficulties and complications.

Today, our enemies are fighting us with the intent of extinguishing the light of Israel, but it will never come to pass. Internally we face difficulties and complications. Part of our nation has become far removed from its roots and from Jewish tradition, and Jewish identity has been weakened. At this time, we are in great need of strong, powerful leadership, faithful shepherds like Moses and King David. We need leaders who will strengthen the people's spirit and return them to their roots and to Jewish tradition, with love and faith, leaders who will fight the wars of Israel with courage and strength, and will subjugate our enemies speedily. By such means we will merit complete redemption speedily in our day. Amen!

Chapter 17

The Seventeenth of Tamuz: The Three Weeks – a Time for National Soul-Searching

We can discern different phases in Jerusalem's destruction. On the tenth of Tevet, a siege was imposed upon Jerusalem. On the seventeenth of Tamuz, the walls around the city of Jerusalem were breached. On the ninth of Av, the city was destroyed and the Temple burnt down – may it be rebuilt speedily in our day. Each of these stages in the destruction serves to teach us not only about what occurred but about its inner meaning.

The siege of Jerusalem and the attempt to sever Jerusalem from the Land and from the rest of the world, is like an attempt to cut one's heart from his body. The purpose of the siege was to weaken and deter the Jewish People through siege and oppression.

The breaching of the walls of Jerusalem was made possible through the civil war that took place in the city. The wall was breached because the nation did not stand united. Quite the contrary, in this war, they abandoned the walls and the city's security.

The destruction of Jerusalem and the burning of the Temple are the result of groundless hatred which smote the hearts of Israel like a plague and ultimately led to the breakdown and destruction of the heart of the whole people – Jerusalem and the Temple.

Just as there are stages to the destruction, so too are there stages to the rebuilding. Right now we see with our own eyes how Jerusalem, with God's help, is being steadily rebuilt. Just as the destruction began with siege, so too the rebuilding is beginning with that siege being removed.

First we removed the siege imposed upon us by the British, who prevented Jews from making Aliyah. Then the siege was removed from Jerusalem, which suffered hunger and thirst during the War of Independence. In the Six-Day War, Jerusalem broke out of the narrow corridor which had stifled its development, and began great expansion. It was united under Jewish sovereignty and now, thanks to God's kindness, it is undergoing a hastened process of construction in all directions.

The siege and the diplomatic and economic boycott imposed on the State of Israel by the Arab countries is gradually disappearing. Quite the contrary, Israel has become among the most successful states in the world, having diplomatic and economic relations with the vast majority of countries.

The next stage in the rebuilding of Jerusalem is the establishment of a fortified wall, corresponding to the wall that collapsed in the past. Just as in the past, divisiveness and civil war caused the fall of Jerusalem, so, too, togetherness and national unity are the modern-day wall against our enemies who still wish to divide Jerusalem and to take control of it. The more we lock arms together, the whole nation, all movements and all parties, with the intent of defending the unity of Jerusalem, the stronger a wall we will erect, and it will repel those who plot to breach the walls of Jerusalem.

And the more we increase the boundless love in our midst, the better we will nullify the groundless hatred, which brought about the destruction of our Temple. Then we will be privileged to see and to rejoice in the rebuilding of Jerusalem, the light of the world, and the rebuilding of the Temple, soon in our day. Amen!

LOVE PEACE AND TRUTH

From the Seventeenth of Tamuz until the Ninth of Av, the House of Israel practices mourning customs in remembrance of the suffering and destruction that befell the Jewish People. The purpose of these fasts and mourning customs is:

> To arouse the hearts to consider the paths of repentance. It is meant to remind us of our evil deeds and the deeds of our ancestors which were like our own deeds now, until they caused both them and us the same suffering. By remembering these things, we can return to the good path. Therefore, every person must take all this to heart during those days, and he must examine his deeds and repent for them. . . . (Orach Chaim 549, Mishnah Berurah).
>
> Five things happened to our ancestors on the 17th of Tamuz and five things happened on the 9th of Av. On the 17th of Tamuz the Tablets were broken, the daily offering ceased, the walls of Jerusalem were breached and Apostomos burned the Torah and erected an idol in the Temple, and on the 9th of Av, it was decreed that our ancestors would not enter the Land, the First and Second Temples were destroyed, and Beitar was conquered and Jerusalem was razed" (Ta'anit 26a).

Today, the manifold causes of the suffering that beset us in the past still exist in our own generation, and we must repent for them. That is, we must rectify them both on the national level and on the individual level.

Moses broke the tablets because of the sin of the Golden Calf. Every generation has its own Golden Calf, our own included. Today, the "Golden Calf" means the worship of money, materialism and hedonism, for some view these things as the purpose of everything. This leads people to forget their values, ideals and ethics, and also leads to their distancing themselves and cutting themselves off from Jewish tradition, from the Jewish People and from Eretz Yisrael. We have to nullify the present-day Golden Calf by returning to ourselves, returning to our roots and to Jewish tradition. By such means we will become reconnected to ourselves, our people and our land.

The communal *Tamid* daily offering alludes to our drawing near as one man, with one heart, to our Father in Heaven. In our generation as well, we have to find a way to unite all of Israel and to bring Israel, all together, closer to God, through increasing the love and faith that is so needed in our generation.

Regarding the Wall of Jerusalem – Jerusalem is the tangible expression of the Assembly of Israel, of Jewish unity. Jerusalem's walls serve to defend Jerusalem and Israel. Unfortunately, in our day the walls of Jerusalem are being breached through all values being trampled and morality being nullified. So far have we deteriorated that there is a march of "Gay Pride" – or calumny – in the very heart of the Eternal City. The lack of an identity and the absence of roots has brought people to confusion and destructive personal decline and the collapse of the family unit. By returning to our essential, human and Jewish identity, we will buttress the walls of Jerusalem.

The burning of the Torah in the past is unfortunately recurring today before our very eyes, through the children and adults of Israel being distanced from Torah study. We must once more learn and teach our holy Torah with love and faith.

Regarding the Idol in the Sanctuary – the human heart is likened to a Temple. The idol in the sanctuary in the heart of man of our generation consists of his anger, lust and drives, and his evil thoughts. We must "purify the sanctuary," our heart, removing the idol from it. By carrying out these improvements, we will be privileged to see the fulfillment of the prophet's words:

> Thus said the Lord of hosts: The fasts of the fourth month, fifth month, seventh month and eighth month shall be to the house of Judah joy and gladness, and cheerful seasons. Therefore love truth and peace. (Zechariah 8:19)

"WHOEVER MOURNS FOR JERUSALEM SHALL MERIT TO SEE ITS REJOICING."

There is a connection between the troubles that befell our ancestors on the 17th of Tamuz and those which befell them on the 9th of Av, despite the distance of days and years between them. The main troubles of the 17th of Tamuz were spiritual and resulted from Israel's moral deterioration. For example, in the wake of the Golden Calf, Moses broke the Tablets, and this was also the cause of the cessation of the daily offering, the burning of the Torah and the idol in the Temple.

By contrast, the troubles of the 9th of Av affected the nation's concrete political situation and their connection to Eretz Yisrael. For example, the sin of the spies led to the decree that the generation of the desert would not enter the Land, and this is true too of the destruction of the First and Second Temples, Beitar's destruction and Jerusalem being razed.

Our sages were seeking to teach us that the moral and spiritual deterioration that caused the troubles of the 17th of Tamuz led to the destruction of the Temples and all the other troubles. As in our sages' words to both Nebuchadnezzar and Titus, "You ground flour that was already ground" meaning, "The first stages of the Temple's destruction were really due to Israel's sins. You just completed the destruction."

During the Three Weeks between the 17th of Tamuz and the 9th of Av, we observe various mourning practices. The purpose of these customs and fasts is to arouse our hearts to repentance, for recalling what occurred can prod us back to the right path.

Therefore, every Jew must take pains to scrutinize his deeds and to repent. After all, the main point of the fast is repentance. "The fast is nothing but a preparation for repentance" (Orach Chaim).

What can we rectify in our generation if these fast days and mourning customs are to be transformed into days of joy and celebration? Regarding the troubles associated with the 17th of Tamuz, corresponding to the Golden Calf, the reason the Tablets were broken, we must strengthen ourselves in faith and in patience. After all, the sin of the Calf occurred due to a lack of these two traits. Israel could not wait for Moses to descend from the mountain. We must become stronger in faith and tolerance on the personal level, and no less so on the national level. We must work together with God to bring the redemption, yet we mustn't fall into a hysterical panic if the process is fraught with crises.

Regarding the cessation of the twice-daily offering, we must become stronger in prayer, our "regular daily offerings," going to synagogue morning and evening, and maintaining regular prayer and Torah learning.

In response to the breaching of Jerusalem's walls, we must fortify the walls of Jerusalem by building homes and neighborhoods in Jerusalem, especially those places over which the Arabs are striving to take control. We mustn't allow Jerusalem to be divided.

In response to the burning of the Torah, whose purpose it was to prevent Israel from learning Torah, we must increase and magnify our Torah learning, establishing more and more Talmud Torahs, yeshivot and Torah institutions and filling the country with Torah. Nothing strengthens and exalts our nation like learning our holy Torah.

In response to the idol being placed in our Temple, it is well known that the Temple was likened to a man's heart. We have to rectify our character, especially regarding pride, anger and lust, which are like idols in the Temple (see Nefesh HaChaim 1:5).

Through these improvements, we will merit the Third Temple's construction, and the return of all the Jews of the exile to Israel. The city of Beitar, which is being rebuilt, will continue to grow by leaps and bounds, together with all the other cities of Eretz Yisrael. Instead of Jerusalem in its ruins, Jerusalem is speedily being rebuilt, and will continue to grow. May we be the living fulfillment of our sages' words, "Whoever mourns for Jerusalem will merit to see its rejoicing" (Ta'anit 30b).

NECESSARY WARS

In this period between the Seventeenth of Tamuz and the Ninth of Av we recall the Destruction of the First and Second Temples. At the same time, we must look toward the future. We must learn, understand and gain awareness that we are at the beginning of the building of the Third Temple, which began with the ingathering of the exiles, the establishment of a sovereign Jewish entity, the State of Israel. All the prophets and sages who relate to the rebirth of the Jewish People in their land after the two-thousand year-long exile, note that the Third Temple will be built amidst wars, as our sages said, "In the seventh year there will be wars. At the end of that period the son of David will come." The nations of the world have not resigned themselves to the idea that our people is rising to rebirth. They are striving to their utmost to extinguish the flame of Israel, that is burning brighter and brighter.

Thus, our wars are *milchamot mitzvah* – compulsory wars. The ideas aired in recent years by political leaders who claim that we are fighting to achieve "peace now" have no foothold in our difficult reality. They are mistaken, and they are the cause of the unfortunate fantasies of dangerous diplomatic programs such as Oslo, the Separation, the Disengagement and the Convergence Plan. To our enemies, all these programs send a message of surrender and weakness. Such plans confuse the heads of the army and demoralize the troops, and are the result of an error in understanding reality.

We are at the height of a *milchemet mitzvah*, a compulsory war, as the Rambam taught: "What is a *milchemet mitzvah*? It is a war to assist Israel against an enemy that has attacked them" (Hilchot Melachim 5:1). During such a war, the people's morale must be strengthened. A Kohen is therefore appointed to address the people during the war, and he is called the *Mashuach Milchamah*, the priest anointed for war:

"He stands on a high place with all the armed forces before him, and he says to them in Hebrew: Hear O Israel! Today you are about to wage war against your enemies. Do not be faint-hearted, do not be afraid, do not panic, and do not break ranks before them. The Lord your God is the One who is going with you. He will fight for you against your enemies, and He will deliver you" (Rambam, ibid. quoting from Deuteronomy 20:3–4).

Rambam also says there:

> When a person enters the thick of battle, he should place his hope in God, who saves Israel in time of trouble. He should be aware that he is waging war for the sake of God's Unity. He should muster his courage and have no fear. . . . Whoever starts to think too much in battle, alarming himself, violates a Torah prohibition: "Do not be faint-hearted, do not be afraid, do not panic, and do not break ranks before them." Moreover, the lives of all Israel depend on him. If he does not do all he can, with all his heart and soul, to be victorious in battle, it is as though he has shed blood, as it says, "Let him go home rather than have his cowardliness demoralize his brethren" (Deuteronomy 20:8) . . . Whoever fights with all his heart, without fear, and his intent is solely to sanctify God's name, can rest assured that he will not be harmed and no evil will befall him. He will build a solid family in Israel, bringing merit to himself and to his descendants for all time, and he will merit the World-to-Come (Rambam, ibid. 15).

At present, we must pray and call to the nation and to its leaders: Open your eyes! Know the enemy and his goals! Fight back hard! Smite the enemy and deter him! By such means God's name will be sanctified on earth. We must be strong and courageous "on behalf of our people and on behalf of the cities of our God" (II Samuel 10:12).

Chapter 18

Tisha Be'av: When We Eliminate the Causes of the Destruction, the Temple will be Rebuilt

Our sages explain to us precisely why we mourn on Tisha Be'Av. "On Tisha Be'Av it was decreed that our ancestors would not enter the Land, the First and Second Temples were destroyed, and Beitar was captured and razed" (Ta'anit 26b).

The spies' betrayal of Eretz Yisrael caused the people's intense weeping on Tisha Be'Av Night in the Desert: "The entire community raised a hubbub and began to shout. That night, the people wept" (Numbers 14:1). The result was God's saying: "Because you wept for nothing, I shall make you weep throughout the generations" (Ta'anit 29a).

The Talmud teaches (Yoma 9b): "Why was the First Temple destroyed? Because the people committed idolatry, sexual sin and murder. Yet in the Second Temple period the people learned Torah and performed mitzvot and kind deeds. Why was that destroyed? Because there was groundless hatred."

Today, on Tisha Be'Av and in general, we must engage in national and individual soul-searching. We must repent in our relationship to Eretz Yisrael, and we must rid ourselves of the weakness and lack of faith in our ability to conquer the Land, shortcomings displayed amongst the spies and their contemporaries. On the contrary, we must become stronger and more courageous. We must learn and understand and believe fully that Eretz Yisrael belongs exclusively to the Jewish People, and to no one else. If we believe in ourselves, our enemies will accept us as well.

We must search our souls regarding our relationship with our fellow man on the plane of the individual, the family and the community, and we must rid ourselves of all groundless hatred, for it has no justification, as its name implies. We must love our fellow man and our people, each and every individual Jew within the nation that God lovingly chose. Through groundless love, like the love between David and Jonathan, we will nullify the reasons for the Destruction, and then we will speedily be privileged to see the complete Messianic rebuilding. With our own eyes we will see the fulfillment of the prophet's words: "Thus says the Lord of hosts: The fast of the fourth month and the fast of the fifth and the fast of the seventh and the fast of the tenth shall become times of joy and gladness and cheerful feasts to the house of Judah. Therefore love truth and peace" (Zechariah 8:19).

THE RESULTS OF ISRAEL'S WEEPING OVER NOTHING

On the Ninth of Av it was decreed that our ancestors would not enter the Land. The decree and its cause left their stamp down through the generations, as our sages said:

"'The people wept that night' (Numbers 14:1): That night was the Ninth of Av. God said, 'You wept over nothing. I shall arrange for you to weep throughout the generations'" (Ta'anit 29a).

Indeed, on the Ninth of Av, through the generations until this day, the Jewish People have sat on the earth and sorrowfully recited tearful dirges about the Destruction of the Temple, the Exile and the troubles that beset our people. And why was that first weeping of the Desert Generation called "weeping over nothing"? Because there really was no reason to weep. After all, God loves Israel. He took us out of Egypt with signs and wonders, and He gave us the Torah at Sinai.

We are likened to a beloved bride, and God is likened to a loving husband and father. At night we recite the words, "You loved us with everlasting love." God, in His great love for us, was bringing His beloved, chosen people to His beloved, chosen land. "The Lord chose Zion. He desired it for His habitation. Surely, He has chosen Jacob to be His, and Israel as His prized possession" (Yehi Kavod).

Yet the spies, in betraying Eretz Yisrael, created a quarrel between the lovers. So successful were they in this that the Desert Generation said, "The Lord brought us out of Egypt because He hated us! He wanted to turn us over to the Amorites to destroy us!" (Deuteronomy 1:27). The Torah responded, "In this regard, you have no faith in the Lord your God" (verse 32). "In this regard" – that God loves us and will keep His promise to bring us to the Land (Rashi).

Where there is no love, there surely is no faith. It is no surprise that the people cried that night over nothing. They thought that God hated them. Truthfully, however, God loved them and will love us forever. Imagine a wife who thinks her husband hates her and is cheating on her and scheming against her. Certainly she will cry bitterly. What caused the spies to libel the Land, bringing death to them and to their whole generation? Rabbi Moshe Chaim Luzzatto explains: "It was their fear that when they entered the Land they would get less honor" (Mesillat Yesharim, end of Ch. 11). Hubris and pursuit of honor caused the spies to part with the Land and to create a quarrel between Israel and their Father in heaven.

Today, we have to rectify the sin of the spies and the Desert Generation by nullifying the cause that led our ancestors to cry over nothing. That is, we must increase love and faith and instill in our hearts the idea that God truly loves us, as we say in the Shemoneh Esreh: "He will lovingly bring a redeemer to their children's children for the sake of His name." Not only must we believe that God loves us, but we must remove the ultimate cause of the people's weeping, the sin of the spies. The spies created a quarrel between us and our Father in heaven in order to rid themselves of Eretz Yisrael.

Eretz Yisrael, after all, is like a mother to the Jewish People. Who wouldn't weep if he heard that his mother was going to be sold? Quite the contrary, we must nullify the divisive idea of partitioning our beloved land and handing it over, God forbid, to a foreign nation. To do this we must strengthen faith and love for our land and our Torah, and we must tenaciously hold on to all parts of our land and devotedly defend it. This is the best rectification for the sin of the spies.

Through such efforts, the day will not be far off when we merit to see the days of fasting and weeping transformed into "times of joy and gladness and cheerful feasts for the house of Judah, therefore love truth and peace" (Zechariah 8).

NEW CHALLENGES FOR THE NINTH OF AV

"On the 9th of Av we are obligated to fast . . . because of the bad things that happened then" (Orach Chaim 549:1). And what are those bad things? There was the terrible destruction of the First and Second Temples. Also, on this day, it was decreed that our ancestors in the desert would not enter the Land. Also, Beitar was conquered and tens of thousands of people there were killed. On the 9th of Av, the wicked Turnus Rufus razed the Temple sanctuary and its environs, to fulfill the verse, "Zion shall be plowed as a field" (Jeremiah 26:18). (Mishnah Berurah, ad loc.)

Since the decree upon the generation of the desert that they would not enter Eretz Yisrael, Israel has faced terrible calamities on that day throughout the generations. The ninth of Av was also the day the expulsion of the Jews from Spain was completed, as well as many other tragedies. One of those expelled from Spain told what happened to his family:

> There was a ship full of Jews expelled from Spain. The owner of the ship cast the Jews out on dry land in a place where there was no human habitation, and most of them died of hunger. . . . One Jew, with his wife and two sons, made an effort to walk, but the wife died. The man was carrying his sons, but he, too, fainted, and then his two sons died of hunger. When he awoke from his faint, he found his two sons dead, but he got up on his feet and said, "Master of the Universe! You are doing so much to make me abandon my faith. Be aware that despite what is being done to me by heaven, a Jew I am and a Jew I shall remain. Nothing You have done to me and nothing You shall do to me will help You! (Ma'arechet. Shefot Yehuda)

Just as in the past, the 9th of Av was a day on which terrible calamities befell the Jews, so today as well, to our great sorrow, in our own generation a decree was decreed, and on the 9th of Av Jews were expelled from Eretz Yisrael, from Gush Katif and from Northern Samaria. Just as in the past, the sin of the spies brought about destruction and exile, so, too, today, the sin of the spies is bringing terrible calamities upon Israel, including the expulsion of Jews from their land. And what is the sin of the spies? Lack of faith in our ability to conquer and to control Eretz Yisrael. As the Torah states, "In this matter, you had no faith in the Lord your God" (Deuteronomy 1:32), regarding which Rashi comments, "God promised you that He would bring you into the Land, but you did not believe Him."

The lack of faith on the part of some of those holding the reins of leadership, in our right and our ability to control all of Eretz Yisrael, is leading them to a hallucinatory policy of "a new middle east," one of longing to establish a terrorist state that endangers our existence, in the very heart of Eretz Yisrael. It is a policy that talks about dividing Jerusalem and handing it over to our enemies, a policy that views expelling Jews from their land as an ideal, a policy whose catchwords are "separation," "disengagement" and "convergence," and unfortunately, not just from Eretz Yisrael but also from the People and Torah of Israel.

The time has come for us to repent, for us to return to ourselves, to our land and to our holy Torah. With God's help we can choose leaders who are men of faith, people of vision, people whose goal will be unity and togetherness. Just as that Jew from the Spanish exile rose up and declared, despite all that had befallen him, "A Jew I am and a Jew I shall remain!" so too in our own generation, we must rise up and call out the words of Calev, son of Yefuneh: "We must go forth and occupy the land. We can do it!" (Numbers 13:30).

"LET OUR SUFFERING NOT DRIVE US MAD."

The Rambam's father wrote a letter to the Jews of Spain, against whom the Muslims had issued harsh decrees. In his letter, he offers them consolation and encouragement, strengthening their faith and trust in God:

> Let our suffering not drive us mad. Let us recall that our covenant is eternal and irrevocable. Surely, He who made it is the God of the universe . . . who chose His people Israel. How can He then abandon them? Surely He gave our people a name the likes of which He gave to no other being that He created [Israel, containing God's own name]. . . . God will not abandon us, neither will we abandon Him. He cannot hate us. Shall a father hate his own son? Surely we are sons to the Lord God. . . . Let us cast no doubt on His fulfilling His promises to us, just as we cast no doubts on His very existence. From time to time, the nations attacking us will overcome us, pursuing us in their hatred, but we will stand firm

> by means of our faith in God's promises. . . . Let us pour out our hearts . . . during days of distress, times of torment and tribulation, days in which sons and daughters are being lost, days of cruelty and despair . . . let us find much consolation and become stronger in our faith . . . let us be reassured of our eternity and see our enemies as a momentary phenomenon, and our future redemption as everlasting. God will bring us joy, as it says, "Gladden us in proportion to the days wherein You have afflicted us, the years wherein we have seen evil" (verse 15). And one of God's days equals a thousand years of joy.

On Shabbat Chazon and the 9th of Av, the Jewish People weep and lament the Destruction and the troubles that have befallen us. In the past, we suffered the destruction of the First and Second Temples; the generation who betrayed Eretz Yisrael perished in the desert; Beitar was destroyed, and the Temple Mount was razed. Over five hundred years ago, the Jews were expelled from Spain. Today, we face the threatened expulsion of Jews – by Jews – from Gush Katif and Samaria. Woe to us over what has befallen us!

Even so, despite everything, we believe and are certain that our troubles are a momentary phenomenon and our redemption will last forever. Our suffering shall not rob us of our sanity or our faith. We trust in God's promise to us: "You and your ancestors will long endure on the land that God promised to your ancestors, promising that He would give it to them as long as the heavens are above the earth" (Deuteronomy 11:21).

Chapter 19
Tu Be'av: Day of Hope

WHY DID OUR SAGES SAY, "THERE WERE NEVER SUCH good days for Israel as Tu Be'Av (the fifteenth of the month of Av) and Yom Kippur" (Ta'anit 26b)? Our sages explain that Yom Kippur contains the element of forgiveness, and it is the day on which Israel were given the second Tablets. Thus, on Yom Kippur we turn over a new leaf in our relations with God and with our fellow man. Such a day is a holiday and a day of joy for the community and for the individual (Ta'anit 30).

Tu Be'Av is the day of matchmaking and weddings. It is the day on which it was declared permissible for the tribes to intermarry, and for the tribe of Benjamin to intermarry with the other tribes. It was the day on which the Desert Generation ceased dying off, and God resumed speaking to Moses. It was the day on which the roadblocks, set up by Yeravam ben Nevat on the road to Jerusalem to keep the Kingdom of Israel from making pilgrimages to Jerusalem, were dismantled. It was the day on which the martyrs of Beitar were handed over for burial, and the blessing of *Hatov U'Meitiv* [God is good and bestows goodness] was established. It was the day on which the Temple custodians would cease cutting wood for the altar pyre. At that point the days began getting shorter and the nights longer [hence the sun had less strength to

> dry the wood]. Longer nights allowed for increased Torah study, thereby prolonging one's life (Ta'anit 31, Rashi).

It follows that this day is one of good beginnings and great hope for the community and the individual.

JOYOUS CIRCLES

Ta'anit 31a records:

> On the fifteenth of Av the daughters of Israel would go out dancing in the vineyards (wearing borrowed white clothing in order not to embarrass those who did not have).
>
> Whoever did not have a wife would go there. The most beautiful girls would say, "Pay attention to beauty, for the essence of a woman is her beauty." The women of fine lineage would say, "Pay attention to family, for the essence of a woman is her children." The homely ones would say, "Make your selection with sincere intent. Only be sure to adorn her with gold jewelry."

The Talmud continues:

> In the future God is going to hold dancing for the righteous, and He will sit amongst them in Eden. Every one of them will point with his finger, as it says, "It shall be said on that day: This is our God. We have waited for Him to save us. This is the Lord. We have waited for Him, and we will be glad and rejoice in His salvation" (Isaiah 25:9).

What connection is there between the daughters of Israel dancing in the vineyards and the future dancing of the righteous in Eden? It is known that the circle is a form that expresses equality. Everyone in the circle is equidistant from the center. By contrast, with a square, for example, the distances change. Dancing in a circle proclaims the equality of the dancers.

On the fifteenth of Av, the day of matchmaking, the noble and saintly daughters of Israel would go forth. Although they were not all equal in beauty and lineage, the exceptional ones would not make themselves conspicuous, nor would they compete with one another or be jealous of one another. Quite the contrary, they would go forth in borrowed clothing, whose white color was an allusion to kindness, and they would dance in a circle as equals, each possessing a trait that the others lacked. Thus, there was equal opportunity for all, and they knew that God, the true Matchmaker, is good to all, and His mercy is over all His works. Hence, "There were no days as good for as Israel as the fifteenth of Av" (Ta'anit 31a).

The saints dancing in a circle in Eden likewise represent goodness and kindness, with "each one pointing at God with his finger, as it says, 'This is our God. We have waited for Him. . . . We will be glad and rejoice in His salvation'" (Isaiah 25:9). (Tosafot, Ibid.). This alludes to the future, when "the earth shall be full of the knowledge of the Lord, as the waters cover the sea" (Isaiah 11:9). When that time comes, all men will know and recognize that Hashem, the God of Israel is King, and His kingdom has sovereignty over all. No longer will there be hunger or war, jealousy or competition. There will be goodness in abundance. The whole world will be preoccupied only with knowing God (Rambam, Hilchot Melachim 12).

The circles of Jewish girls on the fifteenth of Av and the circles of the righteous in Eden have the same purpose: love and faith, goodness and light, and these elements must be increased and strengthened. Through this, we will merit to see with our own eyes the fulfillment of the blessing: "Father, bless us all as one, with the light of Your countenance" (Shemoneh Esreh). May it be soon in our day, Amen!

Addenda

The Story of Rav Dov Begon – His Life, Teshuva, and the Founding of Machon Meir

BEGINNINGS AND TESHUVA

Rav Begon was born in Tel Aviv in 1940 to parents from Poland and Lithuania who had left their families to make *aliya*, a move that ultimately saved them from the Holocaust. His father worked as a physical laborer in construction and his mother was a homemaker. They were never well off, but they were happy because they were fulfilling their dream of living in Israel and building the land. Together with their second son, Zev, at first they lived in Nes Tziona near Tel Aviv until moving to Cholon where the children went to grade school.

Growing up, "Dovaleh" was an active member of the Meuhedet Kibbutz youth movement, and in 1954 he began attending the movement's high school in Kibbutz Mishmar Hasharon, where they had classes for half the day and spent the other half working in the fields or orchards. Dov was active in various student social and cultural committees, and loved to hike, wandering alone as far as Eilat at the age of 16.

In grade twelve he participated in a special program in Beit

Berl where the students debated ideology, arguing about issues such as the value of kibbutz versus city life, or the relative values of Socialism and Communism. He recalls standing up and saying: "We all agree and say 'I believe.' But what is belief itself?" For Rav Begon, this was a significant moment. He recalls: "I didn't have an answer at that time, and neither did they. It took me a few years until I clarified for myself that 'I believe' means that 'I accept and rely on the truth,' but then I realized that I didn't know the truth." After reading about various religions and thinking that there must be some truth in them, he asked himself: "Who am I, what is my identity? In what way am I Jewish?" It was not long before he realized that he knew nothing about his heritage and decided that he must study Judaism.

With these questions in his mind and recorded in his journal, which he kept for seventeen years, he was drafted into the IDF to the Nachal unit, where for the first time in his life he met religious people. On October 12, 1957 he recorded in his journal that after debating theology and life questions with his religious fellow soldiers, he saw that they went to the synagogue, a place that offered them support and served as a "home base." In contrast, he felt that he had nothing comparable to fall back on.

In one of his first mentions of Judaism in his journal he wrote: "After much thought I have reached the conclusion that three things will guide me from now on. Knowledge of the land, nature and Judaism. Why Judaism ... ? I see involvement in Jewish studies – like learning Aggada, archeology of the land, and in general the wisdom of the Tanakh – as something that stores up in a person the wisdom of thousands of years and develops his thought."

In the course of his service he served as a commander in an officers course that included his childhood friend and classmate from Mishmar Hasharon, Ehud Barak, who would go on to serve as IDF Chief of Staff and Prime Minister.

After his service, he left the kibbutz and helped found the field school in Achziv, becoming one of the first tour guides for the Society for the Protection of Nature. His religious stirrings grew together with his connection to the land, feeling revelation from nature itself, and he started taking a Tanakh on his hikes, learning about the rivers and valleys mentioned there.

At this point in his life, he turned to the Rabbi of nearby town Nahariya, Rabbi Aharon Keller, asking what it took to live as a Jew, and he was handed a copy of the Kitzur Shulkhan Arukh (Concise Code of Jewish law), which he proceeded to read and practice. The first time he experienced Shabbat was in Rabbi Keller's home. At the close of Shabbat he found himself feeling spiritually uplifted "instead of being tired from swimming on the beach as usual." He then joined Rabbi Keller's son at Merkaz Harav (Rav Kook's yeshiva) in Jerusalem. He relates that upon visiting the yeshiva he was overwhelmed by the noise, and felt lost in the fast pace of the prayers. With great disappointment he realized that he was not quite ready to move ahead, despite his best intentions to leave the past behind, so he bid farewell to the Rosh Yeshiva Rav Tzvi Yehuda (obm) who wished him well and told him to keep in touch.

Rav Begon returned to the Galil for almost four years, slowly growing in his religious awareness and practice. While living on Kibbutz Gesher Haziv he was inspired to put a mezuzah on his doorpost (out of ignorance he recited the verses each time he passed through the door!), and it was there that he bought his first Chumash and decided not to work on Shabbat. He spent many a Shabbat learning in the nearby yeshiva in Kfar Chasidim, where he heard the shofar for the first time. He wrote letters to Rav Tzvi Yehuda who gave him encouragement. At first he didn't wear a kippah, until he finally dared to don one in front of a group of youth that he was guiding. In response to their questions he remembers telling them that he was trying to investigate and learn about God.

At first his parents were concerned, for they had different dreams and plans for him, but after overcoming their initial shock, his mother said that her father, his namesake Dov – a *sofer* (ritual scribe) and *chavruta* (study partner) of the Ostrovtzer Rebbe, would have been proud of him. Soon his mother asked him to bring a rabbi to kosher their kitchen and his father started asking to go to synagogue with him. For the fifteen years before their passing, his parents were fully observant.

On Sukkot of 1963 Rav Begon returned to Jerusalem and spent two weeks in the house of Rav Tzvi Yehuda. Despite the challenges, he decided to stay, and with patience and determination he remained and studied there for the next ten years. Slowly but surely, the devoted and diligent student progressed in his studies and received rabbinic ordination.

Rav Tzvi Yehuda also introduced Rav Begon to Nava, a teacher and student at the Hebrew University, who eventually became his wife. They have 12 children, and many grandchildren and great-grandchildren. Tragically, one of their sons, Ariel, passed away from cancer at age 35, leaving four orphaned children, and another of their grandchildren Shilo Ariel Weinberger also died of cancer at the tender age of two and-a-half.

MEMORIES FROM THE SIX DAY WAR

In 1967, Rav Begon was called up as a reserve officer to command a unit in the Jerusalem brigade. His first mission was commander of the Notre Dame building with the goal of holding the border line opposite the old city from Musrara to Mamila, and stop the Jordanian forces from entering the Jewish homes. He recalls being outnumbered by 600 Jordanian soldiers lining up against his 40 men, with very few weapons. They filled up sandbags on the roof, protecting their two big guns, one trained on the New Gate, and one aimed at Damascus Gate. As the Jordanians started to shoot, Rav Begon realized war was upon them as they suffered a night long bombardment. At 11 am (his watch stopped at that hour) a bomb exploded near him and blew him a few meters off the roof, but miraculously he came out unscathed. He keeps the shrapnel from the bomb in his office as a reminder of his miraculous survival.

In fact, this was not his first brush with danger; Rav Begon recalls that as a child in 1948, he was playing outside when an Egyptian plane flew over Tel Aviv and started shooting at him, chasing after him as he ran inside to hide. At that young age he had already overheard that his 15 year old youth leader was killed in battle.

Rav Begon's next assignment was on Ammunition Hill, where he was sent to release the soldiers who were surrounded on Mount Scopus. He recalls how inspired he was when he saw weary, dirty and injured soldiers marching and wistfully singing "when He comes peace will come."

Then Rav Begon's unit travelled south to Gush Etzion. Upon arrival they discovered that the Jordanians had already just fled, and he found their coffee cups still warm! He was in the Mukata in Ramallah when he heard the radio announcement "The Temple Mount is in our hands" and he participated in the crying, dancing, and general euphoria experienced by Jews everywhere. A few weeks later Rav Begon served on guard duty at the Kotel during the first Shavuot after the war, and to this day he is still moved as he describes the throngs that streamed to the Kotel that Shavuot.

THE GENESIS OF MACHON MEIR

In his journal Rav Begon wrote: "The purpose that I staked out for my life is to live by the light of the Torah, and to the degree that I will merit to do so, to shine her light on others with love."

In an Israeli TV special documenting his *teshuva* process, he declared that he had decided "to devote my life to education – to teach Torah and love of the people and land of Israel, to both religious and secular youth, to help those dealing with the same questions I once had, and now I try to the best of my abilities to also give them answers."

In 1973–74 Rav Begon taught Geography and Bible in Gymnasia Rechavya, a secular high school in Jerusalem. At the same time he saw many Israelis who came to Merkaz Harav after the Yom Kippur war, searching for their path to faith, and felt that he had to help them and care for all those "thirsty for God's word." He recalls: "When I came to Merkaz I almost drowned. There was no program for beginners. It was like a university, and I was only learning how to read and write. We decided, a group of us, to start a program that could be an address for *baalei teshuva* and all those who want to get stronger in their Judaism in the spirit of love of the people and the land, something which did not exist at the time. . . . . In yeshiva one night we were studying Orot ["Lights" by Rav Kook] and all of a sudden I got up and said to Rav Tzvi Yehuda: 'Lights, Lights, Lights . . . but all the lights are remaining in this room! What about the Jewish people? We have to give over this light to all of the Jewish people!' He was holding my hand, and I can still feel the warmth of his hand, as he said 'Nu, Nu [So, So . . .]' I said, 'we have to do something!' and again he said 'Nu, Nu [So, So . . .]' – This 'Nu, Nu . . .' is what led to the creation of Machon Meir."

WHY DO PEOPLE COME TO MACHON MEIR?

"Every Jew, religious or secular, has a Jewish soul, and it is only natural for a person to return to his true self. Serious people search for their selves and their path in life and very quickly reach the roots. In the end of the day I am a Jew – which doesn't start from me, or even my grandparents. It starts from Am Yisrael, the nation of Israel, the collective. So those who search a little deeper come to learn what is Am Yisrael and what is the Torah and this tradition – it is only natural."

Machon Meir is named for a relative of Rav Begon's wife, Eliezer Meir Lifshutz, may Hashem avenge his blood, a paratrooper killed in the Yom Kippur war crossing the Suez canal, who was a Torah scholar also studying to become an engineer in Machon Lev. This combination was to be a model for Machon Meir's signature approach to Torah that is integrated into Israeli society. "We also wanted a name with light in it – to shine the light on the Jewish People."

Since its humble beginnings over forty years ago, starting off with only a few students gathering in Rav Begon's home, today Machon Meir has had thousands of students studying in its Jerusalem campus. With a sister school for women, Machon Ora, a weekly radio show by Rav Begon, millions of downloads each year from the famous webpage Arutz Meir, including tens of thousands of shiurim and over 6000 shiurim by Rav Begon himself, a TV channel of the same name, and the popular children's channel, Machon Meir has become the headquarters for Religious Zionist *ba'alei teshuva*, their families, and many Jews in Israel and beyond.

Machon Meir: Educational Principles and Methods, in Rav Begon's Words

"We believe that the Torah belongs to us, to the soul of all of us, and to each one himself. Unfortunately not all of us merited to draw from this wellspring of living waters, and so as the first step we have to introduce the people to their Torah.

The first principles are:

a) Love of Torah
b) Love of the people – like Aharon HaKohen – "Love the people and bring them closer to Torah" – but it must be unconditional love.
c) Love of the State and love of the Land, based on the approach of Rav Kook who said "You can't reach the truth of *teshuva* and Torah without seeing the unfolding redemption with our national revival."

"When a new student comes to Machon Meir we usually start by learning with him books of *Emunah* [Jewish faith] like the Kuzari and works of the Maharal, but also the Rambam's introductions to Mishna, Pirkei Avot [Ethics of our Fathers] with commentaries, and of course Tanakh [Bible]. Rav Tzvi Yehuda [Kook] *zt"l* quoted the Mishna in Brachot 'So that he accepts the yoke of heaven first and only then accepts the yoke of mitzvot' as a directive to first cover the foundations of faith and only after he establishes himself do we learn *halakha* (laws.) Only at the next stage do we proceed to Gemara with the goal to achieve independence by learning skills.

"We also have a track for religious youth that went 'off the derech' and are finding their way back. A standard yeshiva gevohah is not appropriate for them. Here we have *Emunah* studies that are needed as a basis. The Machon curriculum is comprised of an *Emunah* track and a yeshiva track. First a student strengthens his faith and then, and sometimes in parallel, he learns Gemara.

"Every student should have a personal mentor, who takes an interest in how he is feeling, and invites him to his home. *He'arat panim* [a shining countenance] is very influential in welcoming a student. The key is to foster a dialogue that clarifies the truth from great openness, and not to try to convince nor to brainwash. We are not learning here for a degree or a diploma, but searching to connect to the truth. It is also important that there are questions that they ask and I am not embarrassed to say that I don't know.

"What is success? As soon as a student starts to feel happy, I know we have done our part. When he knows with confidence what he wants, to know 'who am I' as a human being, as a Jew, to strive for good, to leave his personal ego, to find his direction in life – from this point he can fly and achieve on his own.

"In the Machon there is great love of all people, and the approach is not to separate or disconnect; therefore we are able to accept and encompass the other, and identify with the entire *klal* [collective community]. Every year we go out and spend a Shabbat in various development towns throughout the country, to connect to the people and to add our light to Israeli society. All of our students either serve or have served in the Israeli army, some in very significant roles. We see this as a holy value – a person's value is through his relation to the collective, and Am Yisrael and Medinat Yisrael are the collective.

"We also have a conversion track. I believe we have found a formula for righteous converts that need to identify with the Jewish religion, the Jewish people and the land of Israel. The Beit Din rely on our recommendations and every year tens of beautiful new Jewish homes are built.

"The Machon has become the International "World Cup" of Torah learning. We have a French department that has become the preferred path for young men to make *Aliyah* even before their parents arrive, and Spanish speakers from many different countries in the Spanish department. The students in the English department might be the most open and questioning, while the Russian speaking students are often the most closed and slow to trust, but perhaps the most intellectual group. They usually take longer to open up, like some flowers have a different pace than others. We see this gathering as a tremendous Kiddush Hashem, as Jewish unity ultimately invites the presence of the *Shechina* (Divine Presence.) All the varied groups connect through living in the same dormitories, eating and studying together, but we see even more connections being made when we all go on hikes and together discover the land of Israel through our feet. No one feels condescension or separatism in Machon Meir.

"The soul of man is the candle of God" – every person is a good soul, you just have to light the candle. We have young and old, including pensioners from around the world. We do it for the sake of Heaven and believe that our role is to do good for everyone.

VISION FOR THE FUTURE

"When we started Machon Meir, '*Teshuva* from love' that Rav Kook spoke of was not in the public consciousness, but now forty years later it is widely recognized as 'the way to go,' the *teshuva* that the Jewish people need. There is personal *teshuva*, but we need collective *teshuva*. All of the arguments in society are temporary – in the future we will all unite like in the Exodus from Egypt and at Sinai. We must honor and sanctify Hashem through setting a personal example of Torah together with *derekh eretz*.

"We are full of hope that more and more people will connect to the path of Rav Kook, integrating their physical and spiritual development, both personally and nationally. I am amazed by this country. We are developing on the right path. It feels like there is an underground current, and a movement above ground too, of return and drawing close to Judaism from all sectors – most people respect the tradition even if they are far from it. There is almost no family or town where there aren't people getting closer to Judaism. More and more Jews are understanding that they can't live only dealing with the material aspect of life and are searching for meaning and spirituality. They want to pour Jewish content into their lives. *Barukh Hashem* we are on the right path.

"When the Lord brings back the captivity of Zion, we will be like dreamers. Then our mouth will be filled with laughter and our tongue with singing" (Psalm 126:1–2). When the nations say, "The Lord has done great things for them," we will say, "The Lord has done great things for us" (Ibid.).

http://www.machonmeir.net/